JOHN BIRMINGHAM IS THE AUTHOR OF SO MANY BOOKS AND OTHER WRITTEN THINGIES THAT HE'S FORGOTTEN MOST OF THEM.

He started in the street and campus press before moving to magazines like *Rolling Stone* and *Playboy*. His proudest moment as a freelancer was being published in *The Long Bay Prison News*.

He cranked out *He Died With a Felafel in His Hand* for the tiny advance. It took five weeks. He wrote *Leviathan, the Unauthorised Biography of Sydney* to escape the gravity well of *Felafel*. It took four and half years and won the Adelaide Festival Awards Non Fiction Prize.

He now writes newspaper columns and genre fiction.

If you'd like a freebie, hit up the link below and do as you're damn well told.

WWW.JBISMYMASTERNOW.COM

HOW

WHO
SMASHES
DEADLINES

TO BE

CRUSHES
EDITORS

A WRITER

AND LIVES IN A
SOLID GOLD
HOVER
CRAFT

JOHN
BIRMINGHAM

NEWSOUTH

A NewSouth book
Published by
NewSouth Publishing
University of New South Wales Press Ltd
University of New South Wales
Sydney NSW 2052
AUSTRALIA
newsouthpublishing.com

National Library of Australia
Cataloguing-in-Publication entry
Creator: John Birmingham
Title: How to be a Writer: who smashes deadlines, crushes editors and lives in a
solid gold hovercraft

ISBN: 9781742234847 (paperback)
          9781742242378 (ebook)
          9781742247748 (epdf)

Subjects: Authorship – Handbooks, manuals, etc.
Authorship – Technique.
Creative writing – Technique.
Creative nonfiction – Authorship.
English language – Rhetoric.
Writing – Technique.

Design Xou Creative
Cover design Design by Committee
Printer Griffin Press

CONTENTS

MAKING SOME BANK

PREFACE

The book is called *How To Be a Writer*, not *How To Write*. The former is a practical question, or a series of them. (Do I need an agent? How do I approach an editor? Should I work for free? How do I manage deadlines?) The latter is an artistic mystery. How do I create beautiful prose? Well, I don't know how you write beautiful prose. I struggle to get enough commercially viable words out the door each day to keep myself in truffled monkey butlers and gold-plated hovercraft.

So we'll deal with this beautiful prose question briefly and immediately. Artistic integrity is good, but coin is better. You can't eat artistic integrity. It tastes like sawdust. I didn't write this book to make your words betterer and more awesometastic. I wrote it to help you be a little more professional, to treat your writing like a business. Because it is. If it feeds you or pays your rent, it is a business. If it doesn't yet, it could some day. Writing is a weird and crack-brained business at times, but one you can learn.

In many ways, this is a book about productivity. The catch is you are producing words. Maybe they pay your bills. Maybe they just feed your soul. (Souls are surprisingly cheap to feed.) For whatever reason you do it, if you want to *be* a writer, you have to write, not just tell people you're going to be a writer then spend all of your time dicking around in a cafe thinking about it.

I've been writing professionally for 25 years. I'm still learning how, every day. What follows is all the stuff I wish someone had told me 25 years ago. Looking at it now I've finished the first draft, I can see it follows the same trajectory as that writing life, starting off with freelancing, progressing to books and novels, and ending in a drunken, drug-fucked miasma of crazy book tours and literary festivals. Some of the advice is specific to those pursuits. I hope most of it is useful to anyone who wants to scratch out a living with pen and paper.

The deadline clock is ticking, though. Somewhere an editor sharpens her knife.

Best we get rolling.

PUTTING WORDS ON THE PAGE

CRUSH IT AS A FREELANCER

What even is a freelancer? It *sounds* kind of cool. Like you're some sort of rogue knight, charging around poking things with a big sharpened stick. Things that explode and spew clouds of cocaine and fountains of French champagne all over you.

That's totally what I thought freelancing was all about before I, you know, became a freelancer. Then I realised it was more like desperately grubbing out a miserable existence on the fringes of respectable society and selling the occasional bodily organ to make the rent.

Freelancers work for publications like magazines, websites, newspapers and blogs, but without any of the security of even minimum-wage employees. We are piece workers, submitting and being paid separately for each individual bit of work. Freelancers are not part time or even casual workers. We get no holiday pay, sick leave, superannuation or birthday morning teas. We submit whatever story the editor wants, and we invoice for it. Hopefully, one day, we get paid. Sometimes we don't. Sometimes the publisher laughs cruelly as they light up hundred-dollar bills to set kittens on fire before throwing them in our faces.

True story: one freelancer I know was told she couldn't be paid because the CEO was skiing overseas and could not possibly be interrupted on the slopes of Aspen for anything as trivial as authorising a cheque run.

And then they set her kitten on fire and threw it in her face.

Why would anyone subject themselves to the cruelty, ritual humiliation and institutionalised power imbalances of the freelance life? Because, like desperately poor piece workers in a Bangladeshi garment factory, we are free, if the notion takes us, to not turn up to work and instead spend the day surfing, or perhaps enjoying the ski runs of Aspen. (But like desperately poor garment workers in a Bangladeshi frock factory, we don't often do this.)

Take it from JB. Freelancing is a tough gig.

So the first question you have to ask yourself is, 'Do I even want this gig? Is it too tough for me? Things are pretty cushy here at the ol' garment factory, after all. Do I really want to give up a guaranteed five cents a week and the certainty of regular beatings for something as uncertain as freelance writing?'

I freelanced, almost entirely for magazines, for ten

years before *He Died with a Felafel in His Hand* was published. I was pretty good at it. I'm not pounding my own pudding here. I'm telling you this for a reason. At the height of my freelancing powers, when I was a contributing editor at *Penthouse*, *Playboy*, *Rolling Stone* and *Inside Sport*, and a contributor at about half a dozen other titles, I was trousering about 12 grand a year.

Not a princely fucking sum, was it?

After publishing *Felafel*, when my byline became a product, my income grew and never went back down to miserable penury again. But not everybody gets to write a book like that, and even if they do, there is no guarantee it's going to sell. Luck plays a huge part in these things. And the publishing and media industries are shit out of luck. Google has eaten their business model and the print media in particular appears to be in a death spiral. That can't be good for freelancers, right?

Well, no, but also yes.

This is not the best of times to be paying your rent with your writing. But it's not the worst either. A lot of magazines I used to work for have died. Some of the newspapers aren't looking all that fucking chipper either. But magazines and newspapers have always come and gone. They always will, in some form or another.

It's not all bad news, though. New magazines are constantly opening, the damned fools, and new distribution channels have emerged online. Some of the latter are shit-pot operations run by human pond scum who will never pay you a cent, because that might mean one less bottle of Cristal for them in the hot tub at Aspen. Others will pay per click, which is akin to living on tips. And as the economics of online publishing settle down, and business models shake themselves out, some outfits have rediscovered the radical practice of paying decent money for good work.

Downsizing within the print media industry is also a bit of a left-handed gift for freelancers. For starters, we're cheap. Or at least way cheaper than full-time staff. Freelancers do piece work. Publications pay only for the words and images they buy. As I said before, they don't pay any on-costs such as sick leave, holiday pay, superannuation, income tax, training and, increasingly, expenses associated with research. The freelancer covers all that shit herself. We are the Indian call-centre operators of the media world. Or maybe the million monkeys in Rupert Murdoch's basement. (Update: massive layoffs rumoured for News Corp monkey division.)

What this means is that while full-time jobs are disappearing at a scarifying rate, the low status, uncertain, poorly paid world of freelancing is going from strength to strength. Yay!

There are hundreds of magazines and trade publications, niche titles, which have not been bent over a barrel by Google. They still need regular copy. They still pay. And they don't have lots of full-time staff to generate content. They buy it in bits and pieces just like they always have.

We are a narrative species. We impose order on the

chaos of our existence through the stories we tell about it. Most people are pretty good at this … until you put a blank piece of paper (or an empty screen) in front of them and you say, 'Write it down.'

The facilities for writing and speaking are both located in the language centres of the brain, but they are close neighbours, not flatmates. While most people can tell you a story over a drink, most can't get it down on paper. If you can, give yourself a little pat on the butt. You're special. In fact, give yourself another pat. That felt good. You must work out, right? Mmm … rock-hard tasty writer's glutes.

That's your advantage. That's why you are going to make it in this gig.

That, and these six reasons.

1. The internet is not death of the news media, it is the rebirth. When the free press was born, mid-wifed into being by Benjamin Franklin among others, it looked nothing like the massive media empires which now dominate the planet even as they struggle through their very own extinction-level event. The free press once looked like something a lot closer to the early days of the blogosphere, with an army of amateurs, some gifted, most hapless, doing whatever the hell they wanted, talking to small audiences about the stuff that interested them. That Golden Age of Reportage you heard about? You're standing in its second Age.

2. Yes, a wave of destruction is sweeping across the media ecosphere, but that shouldn't bother you, because you are the small and nimble mammals in this tale, not the lumbering old dinosaurs. Do you personally have billions of dollars tied up in depreciating assets like printing presses? Are you burdened by massive, archaic infrastructure like newsrooms in legacy buildings echoing with the footsteps of ghosts? No? Then tuck yourself in just behind the blast wave that is sweeping over the industry and enjoy picking over the fallen carcasses and piles of rubble. The pickin's will be rich.

3. The technology that destroys, also creates. It was once impossible to set up a newspaper unless you had a lazy hundred million lying around. That's why newspapers tended to be owned by blokes with a lazy hundred million lying around. That's why newspapers tended to represent the interests and protect the power of blokes with a lazy hundred million, or more, lying around. Are you one of these fine fellows? If so, see me after and we'll discuss the large unsecured loan you're about to advance me. If not, then revel in the fact that there are *no barriers* to entering the marketplace of ideas any more. You don't even need a cheap laptop and smart phone – although that would be a start, because with that technology you have more information processing power available to you than

the entire planet could have called on when Rupert Murdoch first published *The Australian*. You don't need a newsroom. You need to get off your arse and go find some stories. Then you need to tell them. People will listen.

4. Your weakness, it is your strength. I'm assuming most of you are young. You have no assets. Little income. Scant investment of time yet in your trade. This is an excellent state of affairs and I am envious of you. You have nothing to lose and a whole world to conquer. You can hazard it all on one throw of the dice, and if you crap out, pick up the damned dice and throw again and again and again. You are not defeated, you cannot lose, until you decide to leave the game. And this game was old when clay tablets were the hot new tech. Don't think of yourself as baby writers or cadet reporters, you are more than that. You are storytellers and the tools you have to tell those stories would have seemed magical artefacts to old Ben Franklin. He doesn't want to hear your whining about Google breaking the business model. He just wants the fucking copy.

5. The fear you sense from your elders is real. Use it against them. So terrified of new media are the old that they forgot the lesson of Obi-Wan. If a News Limited columnist strikes you down, you can only return, more powerful than before. If and when

you find yourself in a death struggle with some Sith
Lord of the old order, remember that their fear is
a form of respect. They see in you their doom. Do
not disappoint them on that score.

6. And finally, remember it is not about you. It is not
about the medium, it is not even about the audience. It is always about the story. You serve the
story now. You serve the truth as you discover it.
You should be most sceptical of the truth you most
want to hear. But seek it, find it, and take it to the
world. Someone out there wants to know.

So, assuming there is money out there to be earned as a
freelancer, how do you get in for your chop? Well I got
some sour news for you, buddy. You start at the bottom
and work your way up. As it ever was, as it ever will be.

SPECIALISE

I'd say that in the modern, post-Google world of publishing, you
should start to specialise much earlier. The future of publishing
lies in figuring out what people will pay for. That might seem a
fatuous statement, but it's not. In the good old days we didn't
actually have to worry about that sort of shit. Because we had
a monopoly over print advertising it subsidised the indulgences
of writers and editors. We'd just write about the stuff that

interested us and assumed a readership would follow. You can't do that any more. People will pay for content, but only the content that they'll pay for, if you get my meaning.

General news, for instance? Fuggedaboutit! If you can get the information free, online, you're not going to hand over the folding stuff. But niche content, especially quality-assured niche content? Yeah, you can still make some scratch off that.

My advice to baby freelancers, then, would be as it always has been, with a tweak. Write, write, write. Write about anything and everything at every opportunity you get. But find a couple of areas where you can ramp up some expertise and start learning the shit out of them. You have to be able to do something that 99 per cent of other writers cannot do. You have to be able to deliver something they cannot hope to deliver to an editor who's buying the story, and beyond him or her, a readership who'll pay for it.

It's not about the art or the craft, it's not about the grand traditions of the written word, or the existential freedom of cutting your own path, it's about getting paid. Never forget that.

PITCH A STORY

So where do you start? Where do you find your first payday? Don't laugh, now. Try the newsagent.

I said, don't laugh, damn you!

I'm serious, take yourself down to the newsagent right now before their business model collapses too. (Most newsagencies now make most of their profits from lottery tickets and cigarettes. You can see where this is going.) Check out the surviving magazines on the rack. Any that catch your eye? Okay, forget about writing for *The New Yorker* or *Cigar Aficionado* or even *Frankie* at this point. They are beyond you. But some of the smaller, more obscure fringe publications are not. They mostly do pay, if poorly. And they are still looking for freelance copy.

Choose your target. Grab 12 months' worth of back issues from the library. Study them. Get to know this publication. Build up a profile of the editors' obsessions. They all have 'em. Familiarise yourself with the house style. Try hard to imagine what a future edition might look like. Those are the stories you're going to be pitching.

How do you make that pitch? Check the front of the magazine. Somewhere up there you'll find a panel listing the names of the editorial staff, the publishing company, and contact details for both. There may even be a line or two about freelance submissions.

If there is a deputy editor, I'd pitch to them. It's a trick I've picked up over the years. The editor is often buried under production deadlines and political bullshit. The deputy editor, or features editor if they still exist, is less likely to forget or ignore your pitch.

The pitch itself should be less than 100 words whether delivered by phone, email or a piece of paper wrapped around a rock and thrown through the window, whatever. If you can't summarise your idea that briefly, you haven't thought it through properly. In fact, 100 words is probably way too many in the age of Twitter.

When I wrote a feature for *Rolling Stone* about street kids I had to pitch it on the phone because email hadn't been invented. (Yeah, I know, just get off my lawn you damn kids.) I rang the then editor Toby Creswell and said something like, 'Hey Tobes, you remember when the prime minister promised no child would be living in poverty by 1990. Well it's 1990 and I reckon I can totes find a few povo kids to write about. Especially if I go live on the streets for a few weeks.'

That's right. I invented the word 'totes' and I was a professional street kid.

Anyway I could hear him levitating at that last bit about roughing it on the streets for a couple of weeks. Editors love it when reporters do stupidly dangerous shit for a story, especially when it's more dangerous than the next editors' stupid shit. It's long been a fave of newspaper eds in particular to send some idiot baby reporter out overnight to hang around with some mall rats and bang out a breathless 1200 words of reportage Straight from the Gates of Hell. I was promising more than that. You always have to promise more than the other guy. And then you have to deliver.

But of course, I knew Tobes by that time, and I could make a very personal approach. How would you pitch a story like that? You might start with a tweet or a short Facebook message. 'Hey, got an idea for a great story on street kids. It's stupidly dangerous but still great. Interested?'

If they're interested they'll ask you to send something through. Expand in an email. Don't bury the lede.

'I want to go live on the streets for a few weeks. Hang out with some street kids, some rough sleepers. Get deep into it with them.'

Depending on where you're pitching you might want to add more conventional elements.

'I can also do the usual interview round. Responsible ministers, community advocates etc. There are lots of stakeholders, but the ones with the biggest stake are the people on the streets. And all we ever get from them are one- and two-line answers for colour in a news story. There's a chance to take a few small risks and really tell their story at length.'

(This story, except focusing on grown-up rough sleepers, is waiting to be written right now, by the way. You can have it, kid. I'm too old for that shit.)

If the editor you're pitching to knows you, they'll probably buy it. If they don't they'll ask to see what you've got when you've run up a draft.

That doesn't mean they've commissioned you. It doesn't mean they're going to pay you anything. It doesn't mean if you run up any expenses researching and writing this thing, you can expect to have them covered. It just means they'll have a look at your stuff. If you're starting out in the game, that should be enough for you.

There are ways to cast your net even wider. There are many, many more magazines published each week than you will find at your local newsagent. Most of them are listed in media guides such as *The Australian Writer's Marketplace* or *Margaret Gee's Australian Media Guide*. All the information you need, not just to be a freelancer, but to be a working writer of any kind, you'll find here. I can't stress enough how useful publications like this can be for someone just starting out in the game. Hell, it's useful to someone like me. So you probably can't afford to be without at least one of them. Besides listing hundreds of publications that pay for content, both have details of industry organisations, agents, publishing services, literary courses, writing competitions and awards and grants, publishing houses and markets for specialist material such as travel, illustration and design. Even poetry.

Get a copy, choose your markets, learn everything you can about them, and start working them like a motherfucker. You have to string together a bunch of clips – ideally on a small number of topics, for which you can become an expert. From them, you put together your career, piece by piece. Every article, every column, every blog post should be a stepping stone to the next one.

In terms of pitching to online publishers like Medium and BuzzFeed, the premise is pretty much the same. Editors of any sort – whether they have money to pay writers, or not – want the highest quality writing that they can afford for their publication. Great stories make editors look smart and ahead-of-the-curve, so feed them ideas no-one else is pitching. Give them a chance to publish work no-one else has even imagined.

If you're dead set on becoming a travel writer, fashion blogger or other niche type of freelancer, remember you're following that passion for love not money. By doing it for love, you'll be able to keep going a lot longer when you're not earning any money. Be prepared to not earn any money for years. Not earning any money is the natural state of being for most writers. And be prepared to work hard at what you're doing, to pour yourself into it, to respect the craft, because you love it. Persistence in love is all.

But get yourself a blog too. Or a Tumblr. Or even a Facebook page. You could use WordPress, or go to a platform like Medium. Whatever you decide, get yourself published before you get anywhere near a publisher. Build your audience. Prove yourself.

And shut up, I know there are 283 million blogs. Mostly unread, and for good reason. But that won't be relevant to you, will it? Because you have some actual writing chops, and you are doing this for love, not for the banner ads or the keys to the kingdom. Are you gonna make any scratch with this thing? Nope. It's gonna cost you time and money. A lot of both.

Admittedly this seems an expensive and roundabout way of reaching your goal. You're writing the book before you're being paid to write it, something I would normally advise against – unless you're doing it for the love.

But you cannot just *decide* to be something. A travel writer, a fashion blogger, a food critic. Well, actually you can. No trouble at all. But the act of deciding is not the act of becoming. The former leads to the latter, but does not guarantee it. Apprenticeships must be served, skills honed, and nowadays an audience gathered and presented to your future publisher with a big red ribbon tied around their appealing demographics.

Be prepared too for your overnight success to take somewhere between three and five years. And along the way you will have to do a lot more than filing the occasional post about your trip to Wallyworld. As a baby travel writer, for instance, you are a traveller first. It is what you must do. You are a writer always, it is what you are, even when nobody else knows that. But the writing is dependent on the travel. To do is to be, as Sartre wrote. Just don't expect anyone to pick up the tab for your existential journey just yet.

Rolling Stone or *Gourmet Traveller* won't commission you to fly off somewhere on their tick just because you ask, but if you have already been there, and you wrote some great stories and captured a few striking images, if you can show that you have already sought out and sustained an audience for your stories through a blog or Tumblr or Instagram, then sure, they might take a look at your shit. It'll only be the work of a moment for them to decide whether you're wasting their time.

Whatever it is you're going to do, just do it. Don't wait for a features editor to send you an advance. Own your love, whether it be travel or shoes, or barbecue legends of the Midwest. Learn everything you can, from whoever will teach you. Then write about it. Because you want to. Because you're good at it. Because you're not a self-indulgent, hipster doofus scribbling prose poems in a notebook at an inner-city cafe.

And be brave.

If you want to be a freelancer – truly, madly, deeply want it – you'll have to get used to asking uncomfortable questions, to going places people don't necessarily want you to be. The best way to acquire that skill set is to barge into the nearest editor's office and demand some work. Or send them a tweet, that would be fine too.

There's just one caveat. That thing where I told you to get a blog.

Yeah, ignore that. It was bullshit, and later on I'll tell you why.

But first ...

DO AN INTERVIEW

Do you know the secret of making out like a bandit at a party where you don't know anybody? Everybody loves a compliment, and human beings most love to talk about the fascinating creature at the centre of the universe: themselves. Once you understand this, you'll never have to hide in the corner at parties again. You'll also be in possession of the secret of the interview. Everybody wants to feel better about themselves. Everybody wants to talk about themselves.

Yeah, okay, I'm sure you can find me some high-functioning sociopath to completely negate that overgeneralisation. But fuck you. You want this advice, or not?

Interviews are not easy. You've seen or heard thousands of them, and if anybody looked uncomfortable it was probably the interviewee, not the interviewer. But interviewing is a very basic skill that has to be learned. It is ridiculously easy to fuck up. Google '29 of the worst media interviews of all time' for some of my faves. You can screw up an interview through nervousness – a particular skill of young student journalists – inattention, lack of prep, over-enthusiasm, lack of enthusiasm; the traps for young players are many. I've tumbled arse backwards into most of them over the years. I'll try to lead you around the deepest, most treacherous pitfalls.

'Interviewing is one of those skills you can only get better at', William Zinsser tells us in *On Writing Well*. 'You will never again feel so ill at ease as when you try it for the first time, and probably you'll never feel entirely comfortable prodding a person for answers he or she may be too shy or too inarticulate to reveal.'

Zinsser worked as a reporter for decades, and taught writing and reportage for decades more. *On Writing Well* should be on your bookshelf, but if you're too cheap or lazy for that, I'll do you the favour of cribbing his notes on how to interview someone. It's pretty much all you need.

That, and a notepad and a recorder.

Use your phone if you want, but I don't recommend it. A digital voice recorder or even an old school micro-cassette unit can be had very cheaply. Use the phone as a back-up if you want. I have been interviewed by a student journalist who forgot to hit record at the start of our one-hour session. I've had my own interviews ruined by gremlins.

I don't want to put your pink bits in a vice, but I will

if I have to get your attention. Read my lips. If you're going to record, use a back-up.

The best back-up is note taking. Use a pad and pen. Learn shorthand, or invent your own system. There is no way you can keep up with a talker in full flight when you're writing longhand. I prefer to write down only those phrases which stand out to me during the interview, and ideas for questions which occur, as they will, during the exchange.

You should go in with a slate of questions prepared; questions you will know to ask because you've done your research. More questions will occur to you as you listen, but you gotta do that research and you must have questions prepared. There is nothing to match what Zinsser calls the 'vast embarrassment' of running dry mid-interview. Don't interrupt the flow of talk with every new question that pops into your tiny mind. This is not an adversarial process. Just note the ideas down and ask your new question when you get a chance.

Unless you're on a podcast, it won't matter if your subject rambles and veers off track. Nobody else is listening. Bring them back gently if the diversion is pointless, but if it is charming or enlightening, give them their chance to run wild. You're interviewing this person because they know things you do not. Find that shit out.

PODCASTS

They're great fun, aren't they. Leigh Sales and Annabel Crabb's *Chat 10 Looks 3*? Love it. *The Self Publishing Podcast*? Really fucking useful when you get past all the fucking swearing. And having your own poddy? Yeah. What a fucking super idea to piss away hundreds of hours a year you could otherwise be writing.

Be not afraid. Everyone gets nervous before interviews, but especially so when you're just starting out. Zinsser again:

> Many beginning interviewers are inhibited by the fear that they are imposing on the people and have no right to invade their privacy. This fear is almost wholly unfounded. The so-called man-in-the-street is delighted that somebody wants to interview him. Most men and women lead lives, if not of quiet desperation, at least of desperate quietness, and they jump at the chance to talk about their work to an outsider who seems to listen.

Most people, remember, are most interested in themselves. You are giving them a chance to riff on that fascinating topic all they want.

When the interview is done, don't fart around typing up your notes and transcription. It is a tedious, desperately unglamorous part of the job, and one of the biggest traps lying in wait for you. Nobody likes transcribing interviews, and we have all tried different ways of avoiding the job. Let me put a bullet into your hopes and dreams right now. Transcription software does not work, not for interviews. Transcription services do not work, not for interviews. They both suffer from the mumbling, discursive, maddeningly difficult to understand nature of the spoken word. The person who is best placed to accurately write up a record of your interview is you. Get it done. The longer you put it off, the harder it will be, and the more difficult you will find it to decipher your scrawled notes and any inaudible passages of dialogue. If you are going to blow a deadline as a freelancer, this is one of the most likely reasons. You put off this shitty chore so long you haven't given yourself enough time to finish the rest of the job.

'What about your obligation to the person you interviewed?' Zinsser asks. 'To what extent can you cut or juggle his words? This question vexes every writer returning from a first interview – and it should. But the answer isn't hard if you keep in mind two standards: brevity and fair play.'

Sometimes they clash. You have an ethical obligation to your subject. Don't fuck them over. If they have taken time to give you a long and considered answer, buttressed by an elegant shitload of context and meaning, you have to do your best to get that on the page or screen. Cherrypicking some colourful line because it would make a great pull quote is a douche move.

Having said that, you also have a duty to the reader.

They have better things to do than read your shit. They are doing you a favour by giving you their attention. Do not squander or abuse it. Most people you interview will not speak well. They will not be precise. Their thoughts will meander all over the page, sometimes going nowhere, sometimes making impossible leaps to other topics, to irrelevant subjects and down dead ends.

You might find some amazing quote on the first page of your transcript, and another line of dialogue which is its logical successor six pages later. What happens to all the crap in between?

It gets cut, unless cutting it would do a grave disservice to the integrity of the interview and its subject. And if it does get cut you have an obligation to get back to the subject and run the quote past them in its new form. Most people will thank you for making them look a lot smarter. If they push back, you'll just have to suck it up and give them a chance to clarify what they mean a second time around. You might get something even better.

I get asked a fair bit by baby writers whether it's okay to 'clean up a quote'? Yes, my little friend, yes it is. But you can't put words into people's mouths. You are claiming to present an accurate record of what this person said. So go ahead, clean up the quote. But check back with them that you have not done some fucking terrible outrage to what they actually meant.

Follow these basic rules and you'll be interviewing like a motherfucker in no time. Of course, then you'll need to figure out how to write the fucking thing.

WRITE A FEATURE ARTICLE

One of the first editors I ever barged in on was Greg Hunter, a great man, sadly no longer with us. When I started stalking him he was the features editor at *Penthouse*, back in the days when they still ran features. I marched into Greg's office, full of piss and vinegar about all the commissions he was gonna give me, and I scurried out with a big sheaf of photocopying. He'd given me the 80-page introduction to Tom Wolfe's *The New Journalism*.

'Don't bother coming back until you've read it,' he said. Hunter was convinced you didn't need to do a four-year journalism degree to write feature articles. You just had to read that essay and apply the lessons.

Let's see if I can do it for you in less than 80 pages.
I'll skip Wolfe's history lesson on the modern novel's
abandonment of realism, and the emergence of narrative
nonfiction as a new literary form after the Second World
War, and get straight to the chocolate.

Wolfe argued that at the very moment literary fiction
was abandoning the techniques of realism, the lowest
form of journalism – feature writing, colour pieces for the
weekend newspaper supplements – took them up. There
were four techniques in particular, three of them simple,
one a little less so. Scene setting, point of view, dialogue
and for bonus points something Wolfe called 'status life'.
Think of it as the description or evocation of social context and you're partway to understanding what he meant.

Scene setting, of course, is easy. It is the description of
the time and place where the story unfolds. For a while
in the 1980s and 1990s you couldn't read a celebrity profile in a glossy magazine without enduring the reporter's
description of their journey through some exotic locale
to meet with the subject of their breathless prose. The
effect can be striking, adding layers of meaning to the
text, or it can suck a golf ball through a garden hose.

The opening paragraphs of Leigh Sales's *Detainee 002*
is an example of the former, good and useful descriptive
reportage:

> Detainee 002 blindly stumbled from the belly of
> the plane into the Cuban sun. Blacked-out gog-
> gles covered his eyes to prevent him from harming

the two crewcut marines gripping his five-foot-four frame. He was a high-risk prisoner, like all the others on this flight. A blue surgical mask covered his mouth, and gloves were taped to his hands. Headphones muffled his hearing. Over an orange jumpsuit, he wore what the prisoners called a 'three-piece suit' – a metal belt with chains attached to leg irons and handcuffs. It made Detainee 002 walk awkwardly as the marines led him down the plane's rear hatch. The hold reeked of urine, human excrement and body odour. Shackled to the floor and unable to get to the toilet, some of the other accused terrorists had soiled themselves on the 24-hour flight from Afghanistan.

Sales goes on to describe the intense and uncomfortable heat at Guantanamo Bay, where even winter temperatures rarely fall below 32°C. She paints a picture of prisoners roasting inside the jumpsuits, weighed down by their clinking chains. Huge, heavily armed marines surround the plane, while 'camouflaged snipers blended into the surrounding hills, and the dull chop of helicopter blades sliced through the air. A gunner hung from a Navy chopper, his sights trained on the prisoners as they shuffled out one by one.'

Sales paints this picture to put you into the scene as David Hicks arrives at the military prison where he will spend the next six years. But the details are also carefully selected to create a sense of threatening alienation, and to make plain without actually saying so the scope of the Kafkaesque nightmare into which Hicks has emerged, blinking and sweating.

It's not an easy thing to do. Marcel Proust will tell you that everything is almost infinitely describable, and then he'll go on to prove it across seven interminable volumes of *Remembrance of Things Past*. You're not going to get seven volumes for your profile of Captain Feathersword in the Toys-R-Us staff magazine, so choose your words carefully. Three pages spent on your road trip with Dorothy the Dinosaur in the Big Red Car to the secluded Feathersword Compound is pushing it, as much fun as the meth-addled hysteria of that trip might have been. Maybe start with a quick description of the soaring fer-roconcrete walls of the compound, topped by razor wire and patrolled by sexy pirate grrrls – but only to empha-sise the emotional distance between Feathersword and the outside world. Then get to the heart of the story: the riddle, wrapped in a mystery inside an enigma, waving a sword made out of feathers. That is your role when you set the scene, to put us in the world where your story is happening, but only describe as much of that world as we really need to see.

There's nothing radical about describing scenery in journalism. If you read the papers and journals of the 19th century, before electronic media became the domi-nant form, you'll find huge slabs of text given over to col-ourful, novelistic descriptions of events. It makes sense. The printed word was the only way of transmitting that information. As alternative forms evolved, newspapers in particular pivoted from description to analysis.

Point of view, the second technique borrowed from literary fiction by feature writers, was more controversial. You'll be familiar with point of view in novels. Crime fiction in particular is famous for elevating point of view, even at the expense of plot. The voice of the detective, his or her world view, is everything. So too with nonfiction narrative told from the point of view of the story's subject.

In *The New Journalism*, Wolfe cites the example of a story about cops, told by the journalist from a working detective's point of view. It reads like a novel, but it's not fiction. Frank Robson is an old master of the form here in Australia. Trent Dalton and Andrew McMillan are his Jedi offspring. A weekend spent trawling through their back catalogues will put you well ahead of your competition.

A couple of picks from my own bottom drawer might help make the point. The first is the opening par of a story of mine run by Greg Hunter at *Inside Sport*:

> Brian looked up from the cabin of his tractor at 10 to 5 in the afternoon and saw the hailstorm which was coming to eat his ripening wheat crop alive. A strange incandescence seemed to precede it. Oh, he thought, this is different, as he turned the machine around to make a run for it. The first stones struck the cabin roof as he neared the paddock

gate, and hail was bouncing off the bonnet like
marbles and Brian Gainesford couldn't see across
the one-lane road.

This is an example of scenic description, of course, but
it's not me describing the scene. It's Brian Gainesford,
of the Backwater Cricket Club. You see he what he saw.
The thoughts and emotions are his, not mine. The next
couple of paragraphs fly around the district, switching
point of view initially to Brian's cousin Mick Cusack,
who was driving home from Cowra and 'could see
something like a giant black hammer hanging over his
town'. (Note the use of the phrase 'his town', not the
more impersonal 'the town'.) We then move to Mick's
wife, Mary. She 'watched it come in from the west,
building in three dark layers, suffused at the lowest level
with that same, strange light which Brian had noticed'.
Mary recalls that when she was a girl, apple farmers
launched phosphorous rockets into such clouds, hoping
to disrupt the formation of ice, while their women and
children prayed. Neither did much good.

One by one we check in with other members of the
Backwater Cricket Club. Willie Kellerman, on his way
home from school, and Mark Munro, who was having
trouble with the missus because she wanted to get the
car in under cover, where Munro had stashed 300 bot-
tles of home-brew. 'The car, he insisted, would have to
take its chances by the side of the house.'

With each new character stepping onto the page we

see what they see. We hear their thoughts. We know what they are feeling. Point of view does not get much simpler than this. It can be a powerful technique for immersing you not just in the story, but deep into the characters who are telling the story. But how do you, the journalist, know what they are thinking and feeling? You're not a mind reader, and hopefully you're not just making this shit up.

The answer is simple, but the practice is hard. You have to interview your subjects. You have to ask them not just what happened, but their perceptions of what happened, their feelings about what happened. You have to go even further than that, placing those memories within the context of the subject's existence. That's how you get details like Mary Cusack's memory of apple farmers shooting phosphorus rockets into approaching storms.

You can expect to do many hours of interviewing for longer, more complex stories, and very few of the thousands, or even tens of thousands, of words you record and transcribe will make it directly onto the page or screen in the finished story. But they will inform that story, they will bring into being the world in which it happened. And they will give you your next resource: dialogue.

Dialogue is not just quotes. It can take the form of exchanges between your subjects, conversations in which you take no part. Dialogue can be internal, a monologue running inside the head of your subject which you have access to by the arcane magic trick of asking them what the hell they were thinking. And dialogue, of course, can take the form of a discussion between the writer and the subject. In long-form journalism, like Hunter S Thompson's *Hells Angels*, or Sebastian Junger's *War*, the 'characters' can talk and argue among themselves across many pages without the reporter interrupting. Or the writer can step into the story, as Thompson often does, and make himself the focus of the action. How the hell do you remember everything that happens and everything that's said? You take notes and you use a recording device.

Dialogue can fill out a scene, or let us into a subject's point of view, but it is also a powerful tool for revealing what Tom Wolfe calls status life: economic and political hierarchies within which the our subjects live. Of all four fiction techniques – scene setting, point of view, dialogue and status life – the latter can be the hardest to understand and deploy, but the most effective in helping our readers get to the meaning of a story.

Long story short, it is how you place your subjects in context. In *Zeitoun*, Dave Eggers takes a whole book to tell the story of Abdulrahman Zeitoun, a Syrian-American who owned a painting and contracting company in New Orleans, before Hurricane Katrina smashed the city flat. Zeitoun opted to ride out the storm. Most of the book, however, we spend with him after the storm, when he is arrested and held captive for 23 days. Zeitoun's story is a small adventure in a larger tale about the militarisation of civic life after 9/11 and the triumph of fear in modern politics. It's a horror story in which we the people are the monsters, and it's made all the more frightening by the care Eggers takes to place the man within his proper context. In the first chapter, we are introduced to Zeitoun's wife, Kathy, and learn from her point of view just what a conventional American family they are:

> There were advantages to Zeitoun and Kathy running a business together – so many blessings, too many to name – but then again, the drawbacks were distinct and growing. They greatly valued being able to set their own hours, choose their clients and jobs, and be at home whenever they needed to be – their ability to be there, always and for anything relating to their children, was a profound comfort. But when friends would ask Kathy whether they, too, should start their own business, she talked them out of it. You don't run the business, she would say. The business runs you.
>
> Kathy and Zeitoun worked harder than anyone they knew, and the work and worry never ended. Nights, weekends, holidays – respite never came. They usually had eight to ten jobs going at any one time, which they oversaw out of a home office and warehouse space on Dublin Street, off Carrollton. And that was to say nothing of the property-management aspect of the business. Somewhere along the line they started buy-

ing buildings, apartments, and houses, and now they had six properties with eighteen tenants. Each renter was, in some ways, another dependent, another soul to worry about, to provide with shelter, solid roof, air-conditioning, clean water.

Zeitoun is that most American of success stories, a self-made man. When the storm hit he stayed because he felt an obligation to his tenants. As Eggers points out, he had eighteen souls to worry about. He was not just a businessman grubbing for a dollar. By taking the time to acquaint us with the prosaic details of the family business, Eggers embeds Abdulrahman Zeitoun deeply in the American mythology of self-improvement through hard work. It makes what happens to him all the more devastating.

There is a postscript. Zeitoun's marriage broke down. He was tried and acquitted of attempting to murder his wife, and has since been charged again, with stalking her. Would this have undermined Eggers' story? Maybe, depending on timing. Or maybe it might have made it even stronger.

FIND YOUR VOICE

I wrote *Leviathan*, my history of Sydney, to escape the gravitational pull of *He Died with a Felafel in His Hand*. Before *Felafel* I couldn't get arrested in that town! Seriously, agents had no reason to talk to me. Book editors would roll languorously in their hot mud baths when I suddenly appeared at their office door with an idea to sell. They'd rub themselves all over with their glutinous store-bought liquid filth, yawn hugely, and pull the velvet rope that summoned the goons. After *Felafel* I was pursued in half a dozen hard-target searches by those same goons, looking to throw a bag on me.

'Miss Palfreyman would like a word, sir, and Miss Palfreyman does not like to be kept waiting. Don't make me beat you with the extension cord, sir. My therapist says I need to cut back on that.'

I could have written *Felafel 2. Felafel 3.* And 4 and 5 and 6. But all for diminishing returns. In many ways *Leviathan* was a return to first principles. For ten years before I wrote *Felafel* I had written feature stories for magazines; that is, nonfiction. There were some magazines such as the old *Independent Monthly* which had a very formal, almost classical house style. Although the articles were all bylined there was little difference between them in the forms of expression they used, in the voice of the writers. A Helen Garner article would read very much like a Peter Robb article or even one of mine. That wasn't an ironclad rule, but it was a general principle. We wrote in a formal style which you can see reproduced in any number of British or American magazines. *The New Yorker* is the obvious example.

At the same time as I was writing for the *Monthly*, I was also filing copy of *Penthouse*, *Playboy*, *Rolling Stone*, *Inside Sport*, *Wisden* and occasionally for the broadsheet newspapers and their weekend supplements. Again the copy for each magazine was subtly different depending on the house style. *Good Weekend*, for instance, was similar in style to the *Independent Monthly*, in that generally speaking it did not allow for any great rhetorical flourishes of slang, swearing, neologisms and so on. That doesn't mean the stories were boring. Some great writers worked on that supplement and produced some quite beautiful pieces of work, but they did so with very plain and simple writing. They let the stories tell themselves, and nobody did that better than Frank Robson.

Rolling Stone, on the other hand, was a different matter. *Rolling Stone* was the magazine where Hunter S Thompson came to prominence. It was the magazine in which PJ O'Rourke published some of his earlier, funnier political pieces. It was not a magazine afraid of correspondents with strong individual voices. Indeed, so strong were some of those voices, such as Thompson's, that you can hear them echoing through the words of a generation of writers who followed them.

If we look at a couple of quotes from Thompson and O'Rourke we can begin to see just how striking the sound of their voices on the page could be, compared to more conventional journalists.

Thompson: 'The TV business is uglier than most things. It is normally perceived as some kind of cruel and shallow money trench through the heart of the journalism industry, a long plastic hallway where thieves and pimps run free and good men die like dogs, for no good reason.'

O'Rourke: 'After all, what is your host's purpose in having a party? Surely not for you to enjoy yourself; if that were their sole purpose, they'd simply have sent champagne and women over to your place by taxi.'

In these two short bits of text we find two very different voices. In Thompson's case he speaks from the black shrivelled heart of a true believer turned cynic. His writing lands on the page like hammer blows pounding his target to a bloody pulp. To do that he chooses his words like a boxer chooses his blows, comparing good men to dogs, presenting us with the alien environment of 'a long plastic hallway' populated not by business people or television executives but by 'thieves' and 'pimps'. His words are harsh because the thoughts he wishes to express are harsh.

The O'Rourke quote comes from a piece about hosting a dinner party in his first edition of collected works, *Republican Party Reptile*. In that particular piece O'Rourke achieves his comedic effect by writing in the very refined, almost prissy style of a 1920s guide to etiquette. You can hear him in your head as you read and he sounds like someone wearing a cravat and nursing a frosted martini. That is the form he has chosen; the content, however, is subversive of the form, positing a moral universe in which cravat-wearing ethics teachers drop pants at the first opportunity and snort cocaine off hookers' boobs. (Incidentally, that distancing effect, a rapid wrenching away of meaning and subtext from the formal text, creates an immediate sense of tension which is resolved when the reader laughs. It is one of the basic techniques of comedic writing.)

Voice is something which can be amplified or turned down. If you're freelancing across a number of titles the switches in voice you'll have to perform can be like moving between languages. If you're still at the learning stage it can be hard to do, but if you've been speaking a dozen languages, or writing in half a dozen voices all your life, you can switch between them without any conscious effort at all.

Let's face an uncomfortable fact. If you're reading this book you probably haven't been writing for 20 years and you are not fluent in a dozen different house styles. You're not the second coming of Hunter S Thompson or PJ O'Rourke. You're just somebody who wants to turn a few quid off your writing. Or break into the biz. Or even just pick up a few tips for finishing your damned thesis.

How do you find your writing voice then?

The same way you found your real voice when you were learning to speak: slowly at first, awkwardly, while making lots of mistakes, some of them really fucking embarrassing. You shouldn't go looking for your voice, you should just let it come to you. In the same way that our accents and our manner of speaking are determined by the home in which we learn to speak, your written voice will be shaped by those places in which you dwell when you were learning to write. You will find your voice through listening to the voices of those writers and authors you most admire. Does this mean you'll imitate them slavishly? If you're a teenage would-be author, for sure. But that will pass. And the more you read, the more influences you allow to play upon your own style, the richer and more interesting it will probably be. With *Leviathan* I eventually stopped trying to force a grown-up voice and just let the story tell itself. There were enough outrages in the narrative that I didn't have to sex it up.

To begin, learn to place one word after another without embarrassing yourself. That will take a few years and your writing will stand out only for its simple clarity of thought and expression. When you've mastered that, you can go wild.

Then you can start sharing your fascinating fucking opinions with the world.

WRITE A COLUMN

By the time you get asked to write a column, you should really know how to write a column. On the other hand, if you're a baby writer reading this, by the time you get asked to write a newspaper column, newspapers won't exist any more. But magazines will probably struggle on, simply because people like them, and magazine people really like them. There will always be some idiot with a couple of million dollars to set on fire publishing a new glossy mag.

What the hell even is a column? What makes it different from a blog? A blog is probably more of a conversation. It's shorter, more informal, and most of the action takes place down in the comment thread. God help us.

It's a mistake to think that a column is purely a comment piece, without comments. Many of them are simply opinion pieces, but some of the best columns in newspaper history were more like the personal diaries of one reporter. A great column was not just some guy dropping his pants and letting his feels run wild. The great columnists took their notebooks out into the city and reported the shit out of it. The difference was, they reported in their own voice and they were allowed to have an opinion. But the opinion followed the reportage.

If you find yourself offered a column, you could do worse than following the example of writers like Pete Hamill, Mike Royko and Diana Vreeland. Hamill and Royko were newspapermen. Vreeland worked a keyboard for *Harper's Bazaar* and *Vogue*. The men worked their cities, Vreeland worked an industry. They all carried notebooks and they filled those motherfuckers to the brim. They had opinions, but they also told stories. They went places, they found things out, they wrote about them.

You can be a columnist sitting in your underpants wiping cheesy Doritos dust from your chest. But you will not be a great columnist unless you get out and work your goddamn beat.

All of the advice about how to write a feature article applies to how to write a column, but there is an increased degree of difficulty because you have to hit harder and faster. Very few columns will run more than 900 words or fewer than 600. You can't bury the point of your column in the second or third paragraph. You need to get it up there in the opener. This doesn't mean you write your conclusion in the first line, but you don't have time to sidle up to the topic. Pull on your writing boots and start kicking the shit out of it from the get-go.

One my fave openers? This, from a TV column I used to write for *Rolling Stone*.

'You people make me sick.'

Nothing like giving the reader one right in the kisser to get their attention.

You will have one main point that you want to make. Don't faff around with a lot of vague, unfocused bullshit. If you have a story to tell, great. Human beings are creatures of narrative. We love the story. But make it relevant, and keep it short. The story is not the point. It illustrates the point.

If you can do humour, good. If you can't, don't even try.

There is no magical structure, no outline or blueprint into which you can pour your words and watch with satisfaction as they format themselves to the agreed word length. Each column will have its own demands, but the core demand is that you provide a discourse on the topic. You don't dance around it. You don't waste precious column length on anything that doesn't buttress your central case. And you don't give a damn about upsetting people. As soon as you put words on a page or a screen somebody somewhere will take offence. That's their problem, not yours. Be brave, file early so the art department can get the illustration underway, and if you get something wrong, cop to it. Admit it. Don't try to bluster and bullshit your way out of your mistakes. You will make them often enough, and if you are a grown-up about it you will get to make more of them over a long career.

WRITE A BOOK

If making your crust from troll baiting and feelpinions all sounds kinda skeevy and gross to you, if you are more of an old-fashioned gent who would prefer that the vile commercial aspects of the publishing business remain, like Herr Bismarck's sausage making, thankfully unknown, perhaps you should consider traditional publishing. That way you need only concern yourself with the need to produce the occasional bestselling novel, and whether to have a long lunch or a late supper celebrating your latest *meisterwerk*. Your publishers will, of course, cover the cost of your lunch, even if it rolls through the evening to become a late supper, and into the next morning to become a drunken, drug-fucked bacchanal with pastries and coffee as the sun comes up.

Yes, that sounds like an excellent plan.

But … But … What are you going to write?

This is a question all writers get asked. Where do you get your ideas?

Answer: the same place you get your dumb fucking questions. Our imaginations, dummy. If you don't have much of an imagination you're never going to be much of a storyteller, unless you have a particular eye for reportage and you're cool paying the rent with nonfiction.

Where do ideas come from? Well, they don't come from sitting around scratching your arse, passively staring into the middle distance. Well, actually, sometimes they do. But you have to give them a chance. Ideas don't form in a vacuum. They clarify out of thinking, and reading, and watching television and movies, and conversation, and magazines, and ditzing around on the interwebz, but mostly they come from *thinking*. Not just consuming media passively, but from watching, listening, and reading actively, critically, but most of all *imaginatively*. This is something that writers should do all the time. Pretty much every minute of every day without even being conscious of it. Actively, critically engaging with media and ideas in all forms is where the idea for your next story is coming from.

'You can't wait for inspiration. You have to go after it with a club.' – Jack London

---

Imaginations are hungry. They need to be fed. Charlie

Brooker, the TV critic turned producer and screenwriter responsible for the creepily brilliant *Black Mirror* (check it out on Netflix) and *Dead Set*, the awesome mash-up of zombie tropes and reality TV's *Big Brother*, was asked where he got the inspiration. Brooker replied:

> I watched a lot of zombie films. I watch a lot of zombie films anyway, which is where the original idea came from. I wanted to make a zombie television series before the *Big Brother* angle came along. I'd decided I wanted to do a series that was a bit like *24* but set during a zombie apocalypse. Then, after having that thought, I was watching *Big Brother* when it occurred to me that that was the perfect setting.

Author of *The Hunger Games* Suzanne Collins also found her inspiration on TV:

> I was very tired … and I was flipping though images on reality television where these young people were competing for a million dollars or whatever, then I was seeing footage from the Iraq war, and these two things began to fuse together in a very unsettling way, and that is the moment where I got the idea for Katniss's story.

Story worlds aren't metaphorical Big Bangs, emerging into existence from a void. Most of the time, like dreams, they spin up out of the residue tumbling around inside our heads. Stephen King has written that the inspiration for *The Stand* came from his reading a news article about the heiress Patty Hearst who was kidnapped in the 1970s by an urban terror group called the SLA. There was nothing supernatural about the story, but it gave King to imagine what would happen if Hearst and her kidnappers were all bitten by a snake which gave them immunity to some sort of disease. From that small germ of an idea came the superflu, Randall Flagg, Mother Abigail, and one of the greatest end-of-the-world novels ever written.

Interviewing George RR Martin for the *Sydney Morning Herald* when the first season *Game of Thrones* aired on TV, I asked Martin where he got the idea. (Shut up, you. If you're allowed to ask dumb fucking questions, so am I.) He recalled he was working on a science-fiction script which wasn't going anywhere, possibly because it was summer and as hot as hell outside, and he felt like he was dying of heat exhaustion. At this point, for some reason, I always imagine Martin sitting at his kitchen table typing in his giant underpants, but I think that says a lot more about me than him.

He told me he was suffering from the heat and the lack of progress on the sci-fi story and he pushed back from the table, closed his eyes and imagined a frozen landscape as an escape from his fetid reality. There was a black wolf standing in his field of ice, and suddenly he was in Westeros.

For Martin, inspiration came in a flight from reality. For Brooker, a story grew from an active seeking, a quest if you like. While Stephen King was idly reading the paper when a strange confluence of ideas sorted themselves into a potential narrative. The only real point of contact between their experiences was that they were all letting their minds run free.

WEAPONS OF CHOICE ORIGIN STORY

I was sitting in the Mitchell Library in Sydney researching *Leviathan*, or rather not researching *Leviathan*, when I picked up Matthew Reilly's *Ice Station* and read it from cover to cover in a day and a half. I loved the hyper-accelerated narrative form he used in that novel and it fused in my mind with all of the historical research I was doing, *and* a Steve Stirling book I had just read, *Island in the Sea of Time*. You throw all of those ingredients together, and suddenly you have an idea for a time-travelling aircraft carrier going back to kick Hitler's arse.

Is there any practical help or advice I can offer to move you through the process of generating ideas from what psychologists would call the day residue (a fancy term for all of the little bits and pieces that flow through our minds while we're awake, often to be reprocessed in the form of dreams while we sleep)? It is that minutiae, scraps of news stories, fragments of conversation, an interesting character who wanders into our peripheral vision as we cross the road, that are the building blocks of our stories.

If I had one piece of advice about how to turn this stuff into narrative it would be to get into the habit of asking yourself, 'What if?'

Depending on the type of story you want to write, the what-if question can be more or less outrageous. What if a woman was forced by an evil Nazi camp doctor to choose between her children might lead you, if you were a writer of the calibre of William Styron, to compose *Sophie's Choice.* What if you were sitting in a big mansion with no ideas for your next book but giant drifts of money blowing around the grounds outside chased by the hundred monkey butlers you bought from Google's special research division? Why, that might lead you, if you were a writer of the calibre of Dan Brown, to re-task those monkey butlers onto blocking out your next book. Couldn't hurt, right?

Having come up with your brilliant idea, but having no monkey butlers to do the initial groundwork for you, what next?

WRESTLE YOUR NOVEL INTO SHAPE

A common mistake of the baby author is light-bulb fixation. The big cartoon light-bulb goes on over your head with a big cartoon flash and Eureka! – You've got it. The idea for the Greatest Story Ever Told (Except for Harry Turtledove's One about the Space Lizards Invading Earth During the Second World War and Getting Their Scaly Arses Kicked, Because When They Set Out to Invade Us It Was the Dark Ages and Now Their Stupid Spaceships are Getting Shot Out of the Sky by Spitfires and It Is Literally Impossible to Come Up with a Better Story than That).

Uh, where were we? Oh right. Light-bulb fixation. Unfortunately so bright is the light thrown out by the big cartoon light bulb (Space lizards! Spitfires!) that you are blinded to everything else. Rushing to the desk, you start pounding the keyboard, still blinking and half blind, tripping over the furniture, knocking over the desk toys and last night's half-empty glass of cheap wine with a cockroach still doing backstroke in it . You type for hours, maybe for days, in a frenzy of excitement because of this great idea you've had for a book … *This is so much better than stupid space lizards and Spitfires!*

And then …

And then …

Nothing. The words stop flowing. And the only sound you can hear is the quiet chortling of Mr Harry Turtledove as he banks another giant novelty cheque from his grateful publishers.

'Nice book idea', he says as he glides past in his chauffeured Bentley. 'Yeah. So much better than stupid space lizards and Spitfires.'

What the hell just happened? Your idea, which seemed so brilliant and unique and close to delivering you giant novelty cheques and chauffeured Bentleys, suddenly seems vague and all but impossible to grasp as it retreats and retreats forever out of reach.

I'll tell you what happened. You exploded out of the blocks and sprinted away as though you were running a hundred-metre race, when what you actually signed up for was a year-long ultramarathon, a brutal, unrelenting endurance event that's as much about attrition and willpower as it is about art and inspiration.

To deliver a manuscript for a 100000-word novel, which is short (at least to me, you fucking pussies), you need to plan for at least a year's work. And that's if you are a full-time writer with all the monkey butlers and a phalanx of Playboy Bunnies to massage your aching shoulders and pop peeled grapes into your mouth while you hammer away at the keyboard. As a part-timer, squeezing in whatever writing you can, when you can … Man, I don't even want to think about that. Why did you even do that? I told you to get some Playboy Bunnies. *I told yooouuu …*

'To have a successful writing career, you must be willing to sacrifice a great deal. The book, the deadline come first before anything else. Writing is not a job; it is a lifestyle, and it is a roller-coaster ride of highs and lows. You need self-confidence and an iron carapace.' – Virginia Henley

---

So, what does planning and preparing a novel involve?

Different things to different people. Not everybody storyboards their manuscript like a movie. I did it with *Designated Targets*, after having got myself into all sorts of trouble with *Weapons of Choice* because I charged in exactly as I described above: *Time-travelling lesbian stealth fighter pilots versus the Luftwaffe? Oh my fucking God! I think I just peed in my pants a little. But no time to change. I must sit here in my warm soggy pants and write every word of this novel now!*

Weapons, as I said earlier, was based on a great idea that came to me in the library when I was avoiding work on *Leviathan* by flicking through Matthew Reilly's *Ice Station*. A military force from our rainbow coalition future goes back in time to give Hitler a schooling with high-tech weaponry – what's not to love? But that was pretty much it for planning and prep. As a result the novel is hopelessly unbalanced. The first 50 000 words describe ten minutes of action. Then you leap forward two weeks and then a few months. There are too many characters, and enormous plot holes litter the narrative path. Still, kick-arse lesbian jet pilots vs Adolf Hitler? You can see why I jumped in. No way was Tim Winton stealing this idea!

With *Designated Targets*, the sequel to *Weapons*, I took six weeks to methodically lay out the plot from the first page to the last. I didn't want to fall into those plot holes again. They're hell to climb out of. Each chapter was broken down into its point-of-view elements (who was telling the story) and summarised in note form long before I wrote the first page of the book. On day 1 of writing I could tell you what was going to happen in the second section of chapter 37, which would probably be hammered out around day 240. Or at least that was the plan. What happened, of course, is that the characters took over. If you have good characters they'll do that. For instance, Dan and Julie were never supposed to get together in *Weapons of Choice*. They were just characters who met on the page early in the book and hit it off.

They hit it off so well that their unexpected relationship became a significant narrative arc through the entire trilogy.

You cannot plan for serendipity but you can sure as shit hope for it. If your characters come alive in your imagination they will do what they damn well please and write most of the book for you.

Does it matter that they won't always do as you planned?

No, as long as they don't diverge so far from the main line of your story arc that they pull everything else off course as well. When you're writing genre fiction, in particular, you need to have at least some idea of where you intend to end up on the last page. It will happen, if your story develops a life of its own, that subplots and characters grow under their own power. But you need to maintain some level of control. Otherwise you end up with the final season of *Lost*.

Of course, in advising you to put some effort into plotting out your story before you write it, I'm flying in the face of the established practice of some very successful authors. Garth Nix, the bestselling fantasy author, has given me exactly the opposite advice, saying that the sacrifice of spontaneity and the loss of the magic of happenstance involved when you storyboard an entire manuscript is just not worth it. George RR Martin agreed, in that interview we did a few years ago:

I've always said there are – to oversimplify it – there are two kinds of writers. There are architects and gardeners. The architects do blueprints before they drive the first nail, they design the entire house, where the pipes are running, and how many rooms there are going to be, how high the roof will be. But the gardeners just dig a hole and plant the seed and see what comes up. I think all writers are partly architects and partly gardeners, but they tend to one side or another, and I am definitely more of a gardener. In my Hollywood years when everything does work on outlines, I had to put on my architect's clothes and pretend to be an architect. But my natural inclinations, the way I work, is to give my characters the head and to follow them. That being said I do know where I'm going. I do have the broad outlines of the story worked out in my head, but that's not to say I know all the small details and every twist and turn in the road that will get me there.

Beloved Australian fantasy author Isobelle Carmody is also a gardener: 'I chuck a handful of seeds into the weeds and see what starts to grow ... I go out and look and see there's a blue flower over there, so I start to prune around it.'

But Garth, Martin and Carmody are successful, published writers of long experience. Most of you reading this guide are not. So I'm telling you, you are much more likely to finish your first book if you invest even a little time in figuring out what the hell you're going to write *before* you write it. It's not easy and there are some elements of every plot which can only be worked out in the writing. Only when you have created and immersed yourself in your imagined world will you understand it well enough to be able to say with certainty how the world and the characters in it will react to certain developments. That's why a plan for a manuscript must necessarily be looser and more free-form than, say, the blueprints for a warp engine.

That's novel planning. How is preparation different?

I guess it's the difference between drawing up the plans for D-Day and actually gathering the resources, the troops and matériel, building the landing craft and transports, manufacturing the weapons, training the personnel, raising the capital to pay for the whole fucking thing, and, well, do you get the idea?

Preparing to write a book like *Leviathan* was not that much different from preparing to write *Weapons of Choice*, even though they are very different products. For both I spent months reading and taking notes, just as though I was preparing to write a very long feature article. I gathered my references. I did my interviews. I tracked down the relevant experts and talked through everything I didn't understand about the topics I was about to pretend I knew all about.

BECOMING A PREPPER

Are you writing a romance novel set during the Hundred Years War? Then, my friend, you have some very long and tiring days ahead of you in the library as you become an expert on the Hundred Years War, on the people who fought it, on the technology they used, the food they ate, the clothes they wore, on the institutions and the states and the personalities involved. And of the vast amount of knowledge you acquire about this topic, only the smallest fraction will actually appear in print. The rest will sit like the frame of a soaring high-rise, hidden away, while it supports the great weight and stresses you will load onto it.

But preparation can go even further than that. If you are setting your story in a purely imaginary realm, you have taken on the difficult task of getting the reader to believe in something they know not to be true. We call this the suspension of disbelief, and we commonly make the mistake of assuming the suspension is the work of the reader. But it's not, it's the work of the author. Your characters must stay in character, which means you must know all about them before you start writing their story. That is why so many authors write long, detailed biographies of their principal characters before they set the first line of their novel down on paper. Genre authors and literary authors all do this. You should too.

None of this advice applies, of course, if you want to be a poet.

BE A POET

Embrace your suffering.

And do your grocery shopping late on Sunday when many supermarkets are tossing their slightly rotten, out-of-date produce.

READ MORE
THAN YOU WRITE

If you can't be bothered reading, don't bother trying to write. You'll fail. You'll be the fat cage fighter whose only training is watching YouTube videos of old UFC match-ups while inhaling a bucket of the Colonel's finest. There's a hundred inspirational quotes from writers for writers telling them to just get on with the business of throwing words at the page, but it's not enough. Before you go anywhere near your own page, you'll want spend the better part of your lifetime poring over other people's.

I'd say I'm surprised by the number of baby writers I meet who tell me they don't really have time for reading. But I'm not. I don't have much time for reading either. I still do it, though. For anybody who makes bank by throwing words around, it's a huge part of the job. Possibly the best part. I mean, for fuck's sake, you're getting paid to sit on your arse and read books. Maybe you're getting paid directly, for a review. Maybe you're just profiting from reading something really cool and thinking, how could I be that cool? But you're telling me you don't have time? What the fuck is up with you that you don't have time to read? Make time.

Every time you read, you become a better writer, even if it's only because you learn not to make the mistakes that make you want to throw the damn book across the room. Example? I've been trawling through David Weber's Safehold series on my iPad and in audiobook format. I love this series, even though it infuriates me. I picked up the first volume, *Off Armageddon Reef,* because I liked the name.

There, I said it. And let that be a lesson to you. Titles are important.

Weber is a prolific author, and I've always meant to read his Honor Harrington series because spaceships and sexy spaceship captain.

But I bought *Armageddon Reef* first, because of the title and cover. It started off 'zactly as I expected and wanted, with an enormous and unstoppable fleet of star-faring space lizards bearing down on gallant little humanity and ...

... destroying us utterly.

Wait!

What?

That's not the book I bought. I wanted to see those space lizards carved up into handy bite-sized casserole chunks. By laser beams!

But no. They defeat the hell out of us and a small convoy of ark ships scuttles away to rebuild the human race somewhere in farthest reaches of the galaxy. Okay. That was cool, I can wait a few books for those space lizards to get what's coming.

But no!

I won't go into plot-spoiling details but the ark experiment goes a little off beam and next thing you know you're reading a ... fantasy novel. And not just a fantasy novel, but one set in a medieval theocracy with a really bloody uncompromising chapter dropping you right into the middle of some arcane point of church politics. Verily did it vex me.

But I stayed with it. As jarring as the transition was, and as much I didn't want to read a fantasy novel set in a medieval theocracy, the Safehold story does become so compelling that more than once I found myself driving a few extra blocks to finish a chapter of the audiobook.

One surviving representative of old high-tech Earth ... er ... survives. A woman, whose mind state is uploaded into a very, very lifelike android, which she has to reformat as a male android because, you know, medieval theocracy. *Armageddon Reef* then becomes the story of 'Merlin' (geddit?) guiding the young monarch of a tiny kingdom in revolt against the hoopleheads of the Church of God Awaiting.

Lots of splodey, lots of running around with swords, and lots of very enjoyable scenes of bad guys with swords getting carved up by a robot moving at inhuman speeds with inhuman strength.

I have but one qualm: a writer's tic that afflicts Weber's prose so much it actually jolted me out of the story a couple of times a chapter in the early books. It's also personally cringe-making because it's something I do enough in my own writing to feel very uncomfortable calling him out on it.

It's characters laughing when they should just be talking.

And chuckling, when they should just be talking.

And smiling, when they should just be talking.

And smiling when there's no reason to smile, because that tells us the character is being all ironic.

ENOUGH WITH THE FUCKING LAUGHING AND CHUCKLING AND SARDONIC SMILEY FACES, DAVE!

Gah!

Elmore Leonard was a bear for this sort of thing. He said the only verb a writer needs for dialogue is 'said'.

That's a bit hard-core for me, but if I could go through the Safehold books (and presumably all of Weber's work), and make one small change that would amp up the awesome to 11, I'd do this one thing.

No character would ever smile, or chuckle or laugh unless they were sitting in the front row of a very good comedy show.

Having identified what was annoying me so much in *Armageddon Reef* I went back through the manuscripts of all the books and ebooks I was working on at the time, and I cut those fuckers like they owed me money.

Lesson learned, and all from reading a series of books I otherwise enjoyed. Your writing can benefit from same sort of learning. The best sort of learning. Pointing at other people's mistakes and laughing at them.

(I kid, Dave, I kid. I kid because I love the series, man. Seriously.)

'You should write because you love the shape of stories and sentences and the creation of different words on a page. Writing comes from reading, and reading is the finest teacher of how to write.' – Annie Proulx

---

You can also learn from writers when they don't make mistakes, whether you're reading them for pleasure, or because you're reading to review. Two examples from my own reading history: a literary apocalypse novel, *The Age of Miracles*, by Karen Walker Thompson, perhaps the best book I've read for a couple of years, and a novel I had to review for the ABC's *Book Club*; and *The Steel Remains*, by Richard Morgan, which I read for pleasure, but didn't enjoy quite so much. It wasn't a bad book; it's a great bit of work. But one of the good/bad things about writing for a living is that you never really get to read for pure enjoyment again. Every line you take in, every paragraph your eyes sweep over, there's some part of your brain which is detached from the experience, refusing to suspend disbelief, because that would interfere with the process of breaking down the prose into its constituent elements. Elements you can analyse and reconstitute in your own work. Things you can steal, to be honest.

Morgan, for instance, is really good at enfolding you within the emotional life of his characters. He's also really good at blowing stuff up. A couple of skill sets which aren't often found together. One of the reasons I read authors like Morgan on an iPad is because of the ability to highlight certain passages of text, append a few notes, and save them for study later. Of course, you can do this with a hard-copy book, but not everyone likes scrawling notes in the margins. I always feel bad about it, even if I'm just using sticky notes which can be pulled out later. Inevitably, I'll lose track of my sticky note pad at some point and start scrawling all over the pages again. Or, perhaps even worse, I won't secure the note in the book properly, and it will drop out before I write the review. My brilliant fucking insight lost for ever.

Not really a problem with digital notes synced across half a dozen devices.

Sometimes I'm just looking for tips and tricks, for simple ways to handle recurring problems. For instance, it's often necessary to have a character pause for a moment while they consider the implications of some new development. This can happen dozens of times over the course of a novel and can quickly become repetitive if handled in the same way over and over again. Consequently I'm always on the lookout for little passages of text like this: 'Seconds ticked away; she could almost hear the clockwork of their passing'. That's a single line from *The Steel Remains* that I highlighted as soon as I read it because of the elegant way it handled the 'stop and reflect' moment.

At greater length, the following passage does really well, I think, at meshing the tangible and intangible when the same character, a kick-ass female action hero, for what it's worth, is confronted with the aftermath of a violent raid on a small village.

> She stood by the cracked and shiny black charcoal angle of the beam, where it met the last remaining upright timber in the roofless house. The sensation surged up in her throat, took her by surprise. The colder, analytical end of her feelings dropped suddenly away, out of easy reach. The ruin rushed her with its silence. Stench from what was left of the bodies in the wreckage around her, uncomfortably familiar despite the years gone past. Ash and less well-defined muck clogged onto her boots to well above the ankle. The knives were a pointless weight at the boot and belt. Smoke came billowing through the wreckage on a change of wind, and stunned her in the eyes.

Morgan has done something impressively difficult in that paragraph. He's managed to embed the character's emotional response to her surroundings within the description of those surroundings. So the smoke, stinging her eyes, recalls for us the discomfort of tears. The pointless weight of her weapons speaks of impotence and emotional disconnection. Of numbness.

This shit is not easy. Especially when you're also trying to move the narrative along with a lot of colour and violence. It's why so many works of literature, which are so adept at realising the internal life of their characters, are not particularly good at creating a narrative with any sense of momentum or acceleration. It's hard. And that's why if you're going to write, you have to read. To study how other people have done it. And to shamelessly steal their ideas.

'Read, read, read. Read everything – trash, classics, good and bad, and see how they do it. Just like a carpenter who works as an apprentice and studies the master. Read! You'll absorb it. Then write. If it's good, you'll find out. If it's not, throw it out of the window.' – William Faulkner

---

Karen Thompson Walker's *The Age of Miracles* has so many ideas worth stealing it gave me a bona-fide literature woody. Specifically an end-of-the-world literature woody. There's been a bit of this gear floating around lately, with the thinky big-L literature crowd finally getting in on the apocalypse act. They've tended to focus in on the zombie meme, although one of the better efforts is Ben H Winters' *The Last Policeman*, about a detective investigating a murder under the shadow of a looming asteroid impact.

Thompson Walker's book appealed to me first of all because of the McGuffin Effect which gets it rolling. The earth slows down. Not time itself, but the days, the rotation of the planet. Imperceptibly at first, but all too fucking perceptibly after a while the days get longer, and longer, and longer. We never see the end, but it's unavoidably built into the narrative.

Told by a 12-year-old girl, Julia, *The Age of Miracles* takes place mostly in the first year of the phenomenon, when things begin to fall apart. Countries, families, everything. Of course, this being literature, misery is preferenced, so it's the falling apart of the familiar and the intimate, specifically the family, with which Thompson Walker is concerned.

Still, it's awesome.

If I'd written Julia, she'd have been tooled up with a regiment's worth of heavy artillery by the end of the second chapter, and expert in five arcane martial arts forms by halfway through the third. Hilariously, my fellow reviewers on *The Book Club*, with the exception of host Jennifer Byrne, bemoaned the lack of action in the plot. It was as though they wanted Michael Crichton to have written it. But *The Age of Miracles* is better than that. Much better.

The thing I love about this book is the way that it

realises completely the world view of its 12-year-old character. The world may be ending, but she is more likely to die of embarrassment first. The collapse of nations is of no real import to a girl who is worrying about buying her first training bra. (Incidentally, Julia's birthday makes her a 9/11 baby. Significant? Almost certainly. After all, this is literature, innit guvnor.) Lest this focus on the personal put you off, let me assure you it adds a weighty emotional punch to the blows that are coming.

Thompson Walker has Stephen King's knack for mixing the ordinary with the extraordinary. I particularly liked this paragraph about the day of the revelation. Julia misses soccer practice, which in itself grounds her within the banal routines of middle America:

> I heard later that only Michaela showed up at the field, late as usual, her cleats in her hands, her long hair undone, her red curls flying in and out of her mouth as she ran sock-footed up the hill to the field – only to find not a single girl warming up, not one blue jersey rippling in the wind, not one French braid flapping, not a single parent or coach on the grass. No mothers in visors sipping iced tea, no fathers in flip-flops pacing the sideline. No ice chests or beach chairs or quarter-sliced oranges. She must've noticed then the upper parking lot was empty of cars. Only the nets remained, billowing silently in the goals, the only proof that the sport of soccer had once been played on this site.

There's a number of things happening in this paragraph, most of them to do with grounding the fantastic in the mundane. But it's her attention to the writerly details that really impressed me. When she says Michaela 'must have noticed' she demonstrates a deft use of point of view. A lot of writers would simply have shifted into Michaela's point of view and said 'she noticed', but Thompson Walker avoided that small trap, and props to her for doing so. I also liked her use of the almost archaeological phrasing in the last line, as though this was a civilisation that had passed and she was reflecting upon it from a great distance.

You can't hope to bring this sort of elegance and craft to your work if you can't even find it in other writers'. I could spend a whole book breaking down novel after novel, exposing the techniques of their authors, but that's not the point.

The point is that if you can't be bothered reading, don't bother trying to write. You'll fail.

NAIL DOWN YOUR WORKING ROUTINE

A baby writer asked me once about my writing routine. Wondering how I get myself 'in the mood' for long stretches of word-smashing. Well, I'm gonna piss in your hot tub, champ. Mood's got nothing to do with it.

Okay, that's a lie. When you're in the mood for writing it's like you're some bad-ass *Matrix*-surfing Neo-motherfucker busting out all kinds of word-power jujitsu on the page.

But most days, you're not gonna be in the mood. You're gonna need some sort of whacking stick hanging over you.

'I could not have written a novel if I hadn't been a journalist first, because it taught me that there's no muse that's going to come down and bestow upon you the mood to write. You just have to do it.' – Gillian Flynn

Rent to pay, food to buy, gambling debts. It all helps get you out of bed in the morning, just like a normal person. A rolling series of deadlines for blogs, columns and magazine articles can also concentrate the mind as surely as an approaching execution. There's a reason we call them deadlines. Debts and deadlines are the real muse of the working writer. Even though you're a writer, one of the blessed of God's creatures, there's a still minimal amount of work you need to get through in a day and if you don't, hard-knuckled repo men will turn up and beat you on the soles of your feet with rubber hoses before taking all your stuff.

I got me some really fucking leathery old manfeet, but I do like my stuff. And if the repo men don't get me, I know the editors will. I might have mentioned them before? The stone-cold killers with flick knives and eyes as empty as the space between the stars? No, you don't want to cross a commissioning editor. And so I gotta work – every day – and so do you. If you're getting into writing to sit around in cafes gently cupping and squeezing your genitalia as you smile enigmatically into the middle distance, waiting for royalty cheques and groupies to magically appear, then get into the fucking sea. Writing's not gonna happen for you.

If you don't have any commitments – bills to pay, bookies to avoid – if you're in the happy situation of answering only to yourself, congratulations. You're fucked. All of your motivation to write is going to have come from within. From your willpower.

You may remember your willpower? He was that dude who told you he could totally get you to exercise every day and stop inhaling whole boxes of donuts as a between-meal snack, and he kept telling you that right up until the moment the fire department cut the roof off your apartment and you starred on the six o'clock news as the 500-kilogram shut-in who had to be lifted off the ruptured bladder of their fetid waterbed by a giant crane.

Yeah, willpower. You can't trust that guy.

What you need is a writing routine. When you work from home, especially when you are the at-home parent as well as a home-office drone, a lack of routine will destroy you. Maybe you're a full-time word whore, like me. Maybe you're coming at your first NaNoWriMo. Most likely you're desperately trying to cram in whatever writing time you can around the hysterical chaos that passes for your work and home life. Even if that's so – especially if that's so – you need a writing routine. So we'll deal with you first, you hapless amateur.

One of the nice things about being a pro-writer is not having to justify disappearing into your Fortress of Solitude to crank out the wordage. But most of you won't be professionals. You'll have to negotiate your writing time, even beg for it. Pro tip: don't beg. It's undignified and signals weakness. If you're serious about your writing, you'll want people around you who take your writing goals seriously too; seriously enough to cut you some slack for at least an hour a day, three or four days a week, to get your writing done. That's a minimum, and it's better if you can find a two-hour block to work in, to build up some momentum on the page. But that golden hour might be the best you can hope for if you're also juggling work, kids, a secret identity fighting crime and so on.

'I need an hour alone before dinner, with a drink, to go over what I've done that day. I can't do it late in the afternoon because I'm too close to it. Also, the drink helps.' – Joan Didion

When you've locked down that regular time, find a place where you go away from the world. Some writers don't need to. Some, like Ray Bradbury, claim to be able to work anywhere under any circumstances.

'I wrote in bedrooms and living rooms when I was growing up with my parents and my brother in a small house in Los Angeles', he once said. 'I worked on my typewriter in the living room, with the radio and my mother and dad and brother all talking at the same time.'

Yeah, some writers can do that, and some writers are lying jerks. Don't be that writer. Admit you need the space. In a bedroom, under the stairs, out on the back deck, it doesn't matter as long as you can cut yourself off and start to work the magic incantations; the ones that take you away to your imagined world. Some noise-cancelling headphones might help, but the thing that will help the most is not laying eyes on any other human beings who have a call on your time. Strangers in a cafe or a library are fine. They can go fuck themselves for all you care. But get away from the people who actually matter in your life. Leave them behind. If that sounds kind of harsh, too bad. Every writer is selfish and if you want to be one of us you need to give yourself the time and space to find the selfish little shit you know is hiding inside you.

In some ways, as an amateur you're lucky. Because you have so little time to write, there's no question of what to do with that precious time when it is gifted you. Put arse to chair and pen to paper – or fingers to keyboard or, God, I dunno, Borg-like dictation rig to your ugly head. Jeez. Do you always have to be such a goddamned literalist?

Anyway, there's your advice. What are you still here for? The time you spent reading this book you could be writing. It's not like I care. I've already been paid.

Now git!

...

...

...

Are they gone? The amateurs? Oh, thank fuck. They're so needy.

Alrighty then. Let's get serious. Gather around, my hardy little word ninjas. You are why I'm here. The ones doing it for real.

It's seems sick and wrong but a greater degree of difficulty attends the building of a work routine when whole days of potential writing time stretch out ahead of you. You could be an accounting student who knows their future lies not in double-entry bookkeeping, but in smashing out double-fucking-plus awesome explodey techno-thrillers. You might be like many writers, a gifted part-timer who can devote only three or four weeks of holiday time every year to drafting up that crime novel. But when you get that time, you are going to own the motherfucker. Or maybe you're the real deal, a full time freelance would-be super-author with a few actual magazine publications under your belt and a commitment from a publisher to look at whatever manuscript you send them.

The enemy of all of you would-be scribblers is freedom. As a writer you have the freedom not to write. Honestly, most days it won't matter if you don't open the laptop, if you fire up a couple of wicked cones instead and play nude *Grand Theft Auto* until midnight. You think Nobel Prize–winning writer Mario Vargas Llosa is at his desk every day squeezing beautiful blood drops of prose onto the page from the single pin prick at the end of his finger? Hell no. I'll lay money on the barrelhead that most days he's ripped off his nut, pantsless, teabagging dudes in *GTA 5*. Because he knows that as a writer, most days it just doesn't matter.

Until it does. And then you're fucked.

'These days for me a writing session is about three-quarters waiting and a quarter writing what I actually want to write. But in the waiting I do write, I just write crap. I just write anything that comes into my head about the character until it stumbles across one of those moments and then it starts.'
– Tegan Bennett Daylight

So how we gonna get you up to an acceptable word rate every day of the working week? First I guess we have to settle on what we mean by acceptable. Victor Hugo wrote 20 pages a day. Robert Louis Stevenson wrote the first draft of *Dr Jekyll and Mr Hyde* in a white-hot three days. Then he is said to have burned the pages and rewritten the whole thing in a week.

Robert Louis Stevenson would kick your arse in a writing slam.

There is a method to his madness, though. Stephen King won't leave the keyboard until he's written 2000 words for the day. Every day.

> If I don't write every day the characters begin to stale off in my mind – they begin to seem like characters instead of real people. The tale's narrative edge starts to rust and I begin to lose my hold on

the story's plot and pace. Worst of all, the excitement of spinning something new begins to fade.
The work starts to feel like work, and for most writers that is the smooch of death.

Some of your genius-level literary types are happy with
a 200-word paragraph, or even a well-balanced line of
prose before skiving off to the wine bar for the day, but
there is a lot of truth to what King says.

Raymond Chandler also testified that he wrote better as
he wrote faster. 'If I'm going slow I'm in trouble. It means
I'm pushing the words instead of being pulled by them.'

The feeling of being drawn along in the wake of your
story, that's what you want. When you're deep into a
book, you dream of it, and having dreamed wake up
with all the characters still hovering as ghostly appari-
tions by your bed until you blink them away. You're not
going to get that squeezing out 200 or 300 words a day.

If you are a full-timer you should aim for King's 2000
words a day, maybe as a stretch goal at first, but eventually as an ironclad rule. Let's start you off at a more
modest 1500. Commit to it. You're going to hit that
1500 and you're going to do it every day. By lunch time.
If you make 2000 you can have a shot of rum with your
lunch and play a little Xbox afterwards. Give Vargas
Llosa a well-earned teabagging.

So now we have a goal to aim for:

1500 words.

Tot of rum.

Humiliate Mario Vargas Llosa.

What next? Do you just sit staring out the window? That's probably not gonna get it done for you. When Haruki Murakami is on a writing binge he gets up at four in the morning and writes for a solid five- or six-hour block. He takes a break to run ten klicks or swim one and half. Then he clears his head by reading and listening to music. He's in bed by nine and up again at four. That's the ascetic approach. Like King and Chandler it's as much about psychology as time management.

'The repetition itself becomes the important thing', says Murakami. 'It's a form of mesmerism. I mesmerise myself to reach a deeper state of mind.'

Don DeLillo has a similar routine. He works in the morning at a manual typewriter for about four hours. Then he runs.

> This helps me shake off one world and enter another. Trees, birds, drizzle – it's a nice kind of interlude. Then I work again, later afternoon, for two or three hours. Back into book time, which is transparent – you don't know it's passing. No snack food or coffee. No cigarettes – I stopped smoking a long time ago. The space is clear, the house is quiet.

None of Ray Bradbury's bullshit for these boys. They create the space and they fill it with words. At the other end of the dial you got Doctor Hunter S Thompson,

whose writing day was detailed by his biographer, Ms E
Jean Carroll.

3.00 pm   rise

3.05   Chivas Regal with the morning papers, Dunhills

3.45   cocaine

3.50   another glass of Chivas, Dunhills

4.05   first cup of coffee, Dunhills

4.15   cocaine

4.16   orange juice, Dunhills

4.30   cocaine

4.54   cocaine

5.05   cocaine

5.11   coffee, Dunhills

5.30   more ice in the Chivas

5.45   cocaine, etc., etc.

6.00   grass to take the edge off the day

7.05   Woody Creek Tavern for lunch - Heineken, two margaritas, coleslaw, a taco salad, a double order of fried onion rings, carrot cake, ice cream, a bean fritter, Dunhills, another Heineken, cocaine, and for the ride home, a snow cone (a glass of shredded ice over which is poured three or four jiggers of Chivas)

9.00   starts snorting cocaine seriously

10.00   drops acid

11.00   Chartreuse, cocaine, grass

11.30   cocaine, etc., etc.

12.00   midnight, Hunter S Thompson is ready to write

12.05-6.00 am   Chartreuse, cocaine, grass, Chivas, coffee, Heineken, clove cigarettes, grapefruit, Dunhills, orange juice, gin, continuous pornographic movies.

6.00   the hot-tub champagne, Dove Bars, fettuccine Alfredo

8.00   Halcyon

8.20   sleep

We all have so much to learn from the doctor, but let's just aspire to his Olympian heights for now. Such practices are only for the gods.

My own day goes like this: I wake at 4.40 am, not because I want to, not because I'm a morning person (ugh), but because I married a morning person. If you find yourself in this very special situation, go with it. As much as being awake at such an hour is an abomination in the eye of God and Man, it does let you get a head start on the other writers.

I exercise. Like Murakami's swim, DeLillo's run, or Thompson's half-kilo of cocaine, it gets the blood flowing. Writing is a sedentary pursuit; even if you use a standing desk – and you should – you're still not moving around much. If you're like Truman Capote and you write lying down with coffee, cigarettes, sherry and martinis, you will soon be like Truman Capote in also being dead. Aside from all the not-dying benefits of getting in some daily exercise, being fit will help you concentrate longer and more fiercely on the story at hand. A standing desk will ensure you don't nod off for an afternoon nap. Especially after a couple of sherries and martinis, Truman.

Although I'm a full-time author, I'm also a parent and the one who is at home. This means that, like any number of mummy bloggers or crime-writing shift-work dads, I'm on point for pick-ups and drop-offs. To be fair, so is my wife who also puts in about 300 hours a week at her office job, but if you are the at-home partner in any arrangement, you'll probably find your morning a chaos of kiddy wrangling, email triage, inhaling breakfast, cleaning house, crisis management and writing preparation.

When the kids are out the door to school I get my emailing and social media checks done as quickly as possible. At ten to eight an alarm goes off on my watch telling me to get my ass to the Writer Cave. I use the ten minutes before the top of the hour to set up whatever music I'll be listening too, open whatever apps I'll need, and beg the dog not to spend the day farting under my desk again.

It's a good idea as this point to do a quick deadline review, just a couple of minutes at most, to keep track of your various ticking time bombs. It's great to be in demand, but as commitments pile up, they can very easily slip to the back of your mind if you don't constantly attend to them. Two or three minutes at the start and end of the day will avoid anything blowing up in your face. You can write out your deadlines in a simple list, or you can get all high tech on their arses with some apps I'll discuss in 'Use the technology'.

'The secret of getting ahead is getting started. The secret of getting started is breaking your complex overwhelming tasks into small manageable tasks, and then starting on the first one.' – Mark Twain

---

Review done, tunes playing, at eight I start the Pomodoros rolling (check out 'Slay writer's block' for more on this method). Two hours later and it's morning tea time. The happiest time of all. I have a cup of tea or coffee, a sweet treat and I read a comic book. I tell myself the visual language of comics allows my written-word brain thingy to relax a little. Like allowing a steak to rest when it comes off the grill. But really, I just like reading comic books.

If you are going to follow my lead and divide your morning into traditional Pomodoro sessions, with a 15- to 20-minute break after two hours, allot a few minutes in the morning before work to set up whatever you'll need on that break. For me it means filling a thermos with coffee, or a jug with water to boil and a mug with a tea bag. If you want a little treat to reward yourself for all those awesome words you just punched out, have it ready to go so you're not faffing around wasting your very limited break time on getting ready to have a break. I even have my comic book waiting for me in my reading chair. These might seem like small life hacks, but it is the relentless accumulation of tiny changes over long arcs of time that will steer the giant ocean-going supertanker of your life away from the giant sucking whirlpools that are always hungry for fresh writer meat.

Another two hours and it's lunch time, which is also the happiest time of all. Again, it's a small productivity hack but know what you're going to eat before you get there. It saves wasted time, and you don't have much time to waste. Not if you're going to catch up with Stephen King and totally fucking pwn Mario Vargas Llosa.

Give yourself a decent break for lunch. You'll have earned it if you stayed on the hammer through the morning. I'd suggest you read while you eat and after for another half hour or so. We all complain about not having time to read, but eating and reading go so well together, and again, if you give yourself half an hour or more a day, every work day, to read, you will starting cutting through that stack o' shame piled up on your bedside reading table.

Of course, you could just get on Twitter or the Book of Face, but I can virtually guarantee you won't get off again for hours. So don't.

By this stage you've worked two whole bunches of Pomodoros. Four hours. You know what? If you're a pussy, you're done. Four hours of truly productive work is about as much as anyone ever gets done in a day. For sure, keep working, but the golden hours of productivity are gone. You're into the sleepy time of the afternoon. I keep rolling out Pomodoro sessions, at least another three of them, but not for book or feature writing. In the afternoons I'll blog or write any columns which are due.

Chances are, whatever long-form project you have on the boil will not be your only writing commitment. If you've made your word count by lunch and you feel good about starting again, take Ernest Hemingway's advice. Give up. At least for the working day: 'You write until you come to a place where you still have your juice and

know what will happen next and you stop and try to live
through until the next day when you hit it again.'

AVOID DISTRACTION

When you work for yourself people often ask 'How do you avoid distraction?'

I think what they actually mean is how do you avoid disruption?

Mostly, you don't. Not disruption, anyway.

It took me a long time to understand this, and understanding came as a revelation that helped me deal with distraction. It was one of those things that seems so obvious when the light bulb goes on. Distractions are always nibbling away at us, whether waiting at home or outside in a cafe or library. Distractions are constant in offices and hard-bitten journalists have long learned to make their deadlines surrounded by a howling maelstrom of distraction.

If those drunken fucks can do it, so can you.

But it's important to understand the difference

between distraction and disruption. Let's take an example that I have to deal with a dozen or more times a year. Writing columns and blogs off the news of the moment as I do, it's not unusual for radio producers to reach out and ask for a few minutes of my time on air. They have a lot of dead air space to fill every day.

When I agree to do an interview on a radio station I might be on air for five or six minutes. No biggie, right? If it's a phone interview that will distract me from work for at least a quarter of an hour – including a little time before the interview to prepare, and to sit around waiting for the station to call, and a few minutes afterwards to get my head out of the exchange. It's a simple distraction, probably forgotten within an hour.

However, producers don't like phone interviews because they can't control the exchange. The sound quality isn't as good as having you in the studio in front of the mic, and since we all switched to bat phones there's always a chance of a drop out. *La catastrophia* on live radio and even a bit of a bummer in a pre-record. So most producers worth their quids will try to get you to come into the studio.

Beware. Disruption ahead.

By the time I've driven through the city, parked, dealt with security, done the interview, extracted myself and driven home, I was still on air for only five or six minutes, but there's a giant fucking asteroid crater sitting in the middle of my work day. You can try to work around it. Get stuff done in the morning. Get more stuff done in the afternoon. Let go of any frustration in between. But by agreeing to the station's request (which can sound very much like the world's most reasonable demand coming from a good producer), I have cratered my day.

Chances are I won't write a line worth shit.

WHERE DISRUPTION LURKS

You might not get a lot of calls from radio producers, but the world is full of scheming maenads looking to bring chaos to your writing routine. Family needing you to do something for 'just a few minutes'. Friends who want to catch up for quick coffee and can't believe you're not free. What the hell? You have the whole day to yourself! Important meetings with important people who are much more important than the 1500 words you promised to write before lunch time. Errands which have piled up and which would only require a quick trip out to the shops for half an hour. And while you're there, you could have that coffee with your friend. And what the hell, if you're away from the desk why not take that important meeting with that important person, even if it's on the other side of the city. You're already out there, after all.

Here's the hard truth. Any time you unchain yourself from writing for more than ten minutes you invite massive disruption to your day. If you think you can be away for an hour because you still have all the hours of the day to play with, you're wrong. Commit to the writing and get it done. Take no meetings, no phone calls, no catch ups with louche friends, not during your golden writing hours.

And saying no to disruption, you will learn to ignore distraction. Because distraction is entirely and easily avoidable. Distraction is your Xbox. Or Twitter. Or faffing about jumping from one nude celebrity website to another. 'A writer', says Don DeLillo, 'takes earnest measures to secure his solitude and then finds endless ways to squander it. Looking out the window, reading random entries in the dictionary.'

Testify, brother.

In an office, distraction is a productivity cancer. It can eat your entire day if you let it. Emails, Slack chat windows, phone calls, pop-in visits to your desk. A long line of people looking to steal five minutes here, ten minutes there. As a writer you shouldn't have to suffer any of that shit, because you can and should unplug and turn it all off.

I return here to your time-management technique, whether it's some variation of the Pomodoro method (which I will totally get to very soon, promise) or something simpler, and harder, like Murakami or Stephen King strapping themselves into the writing chair for a solid four or five hours. When you're writing, you write. Don't do anything else. Don't even jump across to Wikipedia to research some crucial factoid. You'll fall down the rabbit hole and five hours later you'll emerge from a Facebook binge with nothing to show for the day but a terrible sickness of the soul. The factoid can be researched later. Leave a note in the text to that effect.

Dividing your creative time into Pomodoro sessions will help control the cravings for distraction, because you only have to fend them off for a short time. You can even use distraction to your advantage. Promise yourself a solid binge of time-wasting after you've made your word quota. You'll be surprised how little attraction it holds when you don't have a deadline.

One final note about distraction and disruption. The devil takes on an especially insidious form when he comes garbed in the raiment of the righteous.

What the fuck does that mean?

It means you might be an All Star when it comes to not playing Xbox or chasing the cat around the house on a Roomba when you should be writing. But what about allowing your carefully thought out writing routine to be demolished by ... writing. Not just emails or blog posts or tweets or Facebook updates. But real writing. Paying gigs?

This is not just a question for writers who've levelled up to Legendary Status and find themselves showered with shiny baubles and fat commissions from fashion magazines. Grubbing freelancers at the start of their careers need to recognise the difference between work that's important and work that's urgent.

The urgent always wants to push out the important, but over the long arc the writing you deem as being more important to you is ... well ... what do you fucking think?

Dwight D Eisenhower, the general who kicked Hitler's arse and went on to become President of the United States, once said, 'I have two kinds of problems: the urgent and the important'. He added that they were rarely the same thing. Eisenhower organised his work by grouping it into four categories:

1. important and urgent

2. important but not urgent

3. not important but urgent

4. not important and not urgent.

Eisenhower used this formula to beat the Nazis and lead an emergent superpower. You can totally use it to get your novel written, or your blog to a thousand hits a day, or your freelance business into profit. It is a weirdly effective way for writers to sort the bullshit from the burritos.

Let's take them one by one.

IMPORTANT AND URGENT

Writing jobs that are both important and urgent don't all come as sneak attacks. Just ask George RR Martin. As the narrative arcs of the *Game of Thrones* TV series reached out and bent towards the point at which he'd left *A Dance with Dragons*, the delivery of his next tome, *The Winds of Winter*, became both unbearably urgent and important. But that had been coming for years.

Martin blamed the slippage on busy scheduling, distractions and, most tellingly, on writer's block. (You never, ever admit to writer's block. It's like confessing to impotence. It's naming the devil. It's perdition and damnation.)

'I won't make excuses', he wrote on his blog, announcing that the book would not be ready in time. 'There are no excuses. No-one else is to blame. Not my editors and publishers, not HBO. It's on me. I tried, and I am still trying.'

Oh man, I felt for him, and you should too if you call yourself a writer. But you should also learn from his failure. These foreseeable crises, these terrible but predictable train wrecks of clashing urgency and importance, they are the worst. One of the reasons we 'suddenly' get buried by deadlines that are both urgent and important is by not planning to meet them, by not giving ourselves enough time, by fuck-knuckling around like utter arse-clowns as the due date stalks closer. I've been there. You've been or will be. We can both do better.

One piece of advice, besides staying off Facebook

and Xbox? Honestly assess how much time you need to finish a project, then add a buffer. Thirty per cent should see you right. Ten will scare the bejesus out of everyone involved because you will totally blow it or come so close as makes no difference.

The other sort of urgent and important crisis really is an ambush, something that arises without notice. I had one today while I hammered away at this very book; a request from a newspaper to write a column they desperately needed and wanted. Two-hour deadline. Top-shelf pay day. It's the sort of request to which you want to say yes, because they'll owe you one. I said yes because I needed the money.

There are some things which can't be avoided. Bookies you owe. Sick family members. Really good cat videos on the internet. No, like really fucking good. Again, building a buffer into your longer, important projects will leave you time to deal with these.

IMPORTANT BUT NOT URGENT

These are the books and stories you should be writing every day, so they don't have a chance to become urgent. This is the novel you're going to enter into the competition for unpublished writers, not this year, but next. Because you're going to give yourself time to do it properly.

This is the daily grind of building up your blog. Sure, you can miss a day's posting, but don't. Because the pressure will come on the next day, and you'll feel it and if your cat rides the fucking Roomba off the fourth-floor balcony you'll probably miss that day too, and then you'll be throwing any old shit at the screen just for the clicks. Because you urgently need the clicks.

This is that feature commission you've been chasing, in the glossy magazine that still has adverts and pays expenses and lets you invoice at a buck-fifty a word. Sure, print schedules mean you've got three months before you have to file copy, but that doesn't mean you have two and a half months to sit around scratching your arse. Get on it now, you lazy slug.

The most important writing you'll ever do is the writing you look back on with pride at the end of your career and know that even though you let that cat launch itself off the balcony on a Roomba which totally wasn't designed for that shit, you still did alright by the world.

You need to do that writing every day. Even if it's only for an hour.

NOT IMPORTANT BUT URGENT

This category could easily be filed under Other People's Shit, because that's almost invariably what it is.

Other people will have priorities that might be of world-ending importance to them. That doesn't make them your priority, and yet so much of our days, and certainly our email traffic, are taken up by the witless hysteria of oxygen thieves sucking the air out of our day. I count any invitation from government department to attend anything other than the presentation of a giant novelty cheque to yours truly as among the worst of these abuses. Although invites to poetry slams aren't far behind.

The easiest way of avoiding these entanglements is to practise saying no.

NOT IMPORTANT, NOT URGENT

These are the traps we lay for ourselves. The little distractions that become disruptions.

Example? The former Wallaby turned popular historian Peter FitzSimons once told me he used to have a copy of a terrible 8-bit submarine-hunting game on his laptop. He wrote a lot more books after deleting that thing than he ever managed before getting rid of it.

I tell people that *Leviathan* took four and half years to write, and I do not lie. But three of those years went into a hole at the bottom of which you'd find me, Gollum-like, giving myself an RSI playing *Diablo* on an old MacBook. That award-winning work was written only after I deleted the files and smashed the game disks.

You will have dozens of unimportant, bullshit time wasters in your life that you could delete to create more time for reading and writing … if you really wanted to be a writer. But what if you are a writer and time itself is crushing the life out of you?

SLAY WRITER'S BLOCK

Writer's block? No way. I don't have it, never get it. It's not a problem, oh dear me no. Heaven forfend.

That doesn't mean however that I don't occasionally stare at the screen with a big dollop of spittle oozing out of my mouth, motionless hands lying on the keyboard like a couple of dead skinless rats. It doesn't mean I don't get distracted by YouTube, or Fail Blog, or nude celebrity Tumblrs, or whatever fine piece of infotainment is currently oozing from the bunghole of TVSN like a sentient slime mould.

But that's not writer's block, that's weakness and laziness, and the remedy, according to Philip Pullman, is a big ol' mug of harden the fuck up.

Writer's block ... a lot of howling nonsense would be avoided if, in every sentence containing the word WRITER, that word was taken out and the word PLUMBER substituted; and the result examined for the sense it makes. Do plumbers get plumber's block? What would you think of a plumber who used that as an excuse not to do any work that day?

The fact is that writing is hard work, and sometimes you don't want to do it, and you can't think of what to write next, and you're fed up with the whole damn business. Do you think plumbers don't feel like that about their work from time to time? Of course there will be days when the stuff is not flowing freely. What you do then is MAKE IT UP ...

Pullman's full of shit, of course. Hard-knuckled professional writers do get blocked. Some poor bastards get it something terrible, sometimes for the simplest of reasons. Jim Minz, the US editor/publisher on *Final Impact*, told me a story about a very famous US sci-fi author who suffered crippling writer's block for two or three years after he gave up smoking. Having a lit cigarette beside his keyboard or typewriter was such an important part of his productive ritual that taking it away meant taking away his ability to tell stories.

For me writer's block is less an issue than 'going tharn', a phrase from the old *Watership Down* novel to explain what happens to a rabbit when it stops in the middle of the road transfixed by the onrushing headlights of a car. Deadlines can be like that. Sometimes they can come at you so quickly, with such a thunderous world-ending roar, that you feel as though you are paralysed, when really all you have to do is put one tiny rabbit's paw in front of the other and get your furry little arse on the move.

And that finally brings us back to the Pomodoro technique, a productivity hack I turned to after a couple of weeks' dissatisfaction with my daily productivity. It was a few years ago and I'd just come off a book tour. I was having trouble getting back into the grind. I didn't seem to be getting anywhere and the deadlines were starting to plow me under.

Bottom line, I had too much work and too little time and focus. The modern condition. And a lot of that work was long form – books and lengthy magazine articles. Trying to mash them in around blog and column commitments simply wasn't working out. Schedules slipped. Deadlines piled up. I started to see editors following me on the street, casually picking at their teeth with flick knives.

So of course I procrastinated. But I procrastinated like a boss, investing a couple of hours faffing around on the net looking for articles about time management and, sure, getting in some nude celebrity Tumblr time. A guy's gotta live, you know. Eventually I found a useful piece on attention span training at Lifehacker – a link to a site set up by Francesco Cirillo, the patron saint of procrastinating hoopleheads. Poor Franco was a first-year university student with an attention span so short he couldn't even make ten minutes of study. In desperation, and not a little shame, he came up with a time-management system that has saved millions of people even lazier than first-year university students. The only timer Franco had to hand was one of those cool red plastic tomato timer thingies. Hence the name of his time-management cult: the Pomodoro technique.

There is a guidebook, easily findable online, that runs to about 40 pages, but I'll see if I can explain it in a paragraph. Rather than thinking of your day as a whole day, or even two halves, Franco's standard unit of time, a Pomodoro, is only half an hour. Probably because those nifty tomato-shaped kitchen timer thingies work in half-hour blocks. Of that half hour, 25 minutes is pure work, and five minutes is rest. Yeah, you get work credit for sitting on your arse doing nothing. You can see why this appealed to me straight off.

You start your day by reviewing your activities list, which in my case right now would have five ebooks, two novels and a bunch of other smaller writing jobs on it. You cherrypick this list for your *Today* list. Then you simply start at the top of the list and work through it in bite-sized chunks; Pomodoro bite-sized chunks. Twenty-five minutes on, five minutes off. Put four of those deadline-torching mofos together then take a longer, 15-minute break. Rinse and repeat and wait for the literary awards and the fat royalties to start rolling.

There *is* a little bit of planning and account keeping to track your time – and let me tell you, the first day or two that you do that, it's fucking terrifying and humiliating to realise how much of your day you waste fuck-knuckling around. But the Pomodoro technique knows you and your sneaky fuck-knuckling ways. The main thing about a Pomodoro? It is indivisible. It's the subatomic particle of time management. Once you start working on your Pomo you cannot interrupt it, not without abandoning that Pomodoro altogether and being unable to record it as a completed session. You'll be surprised how much of a motivation that becomes to not check your email or Twitter or to answer the phone.

Granted, there's nothing remotely romantic or literary about dividing your day up the way lawyers carve theirs into six-minute sushi chunks. But suck it up, princess. You wanted to be a writer, so now you're stuck with writing, and committing to something like the Pomodoro technique means that when you place arse to Aeron chair you're not thinking about the crushing tsunami of unwritten words that's about to plow you under. You're only thinking about spooning out 25 minutes before you get up, stretch and maybe give the dog a bit of a scratch behind the ear. Unless she's been farting under your workbench, of course. Damned dog.

'Imagine that you are dying. If you had a terminal disease would you finish this book? Why not? The thing that annoys this 10-weeks-to-live self is the thing that is wrong with the book. So change it. Stop arguing with yourself. Change it. See? Easy. And no-one had to die.' – Anne Enright

So, for those of you with looming deadlines, be they manuscripts or assignments or just a bit of fan fiction you wanted to get done, don't think about the deadline or the impossible amount of work you have to get through to meet it. Just think about the very small amount of work you have directly in front of you. One screen, one page. One line. That's all you're thinking about. There is an old saying which applies here: 'Don't try to eat the elephant in one bite'.

If that fails, however, if you find yourself bleeding from the eyeballs, staring at a screen or a page which just won't fill up with magic words, if all of your beautiful little word fairies have died, or hit the crack pipe hard and now they're on the corner waving soiled underpants at passing motorists and offering toothless blowjobs for two bucks, if you really, really, really can't break the block, if editors and publishers are scratching at the door like fiends from the seventh level of hell, well, there are still a few last desperate plays to make.

Change it up. It might be time to get out of your writer cave and emerge into the bright, scorching light of day – *Oh God, the light, it burns, it burns so much.* Maybe like me you have a beautiful, architecturally designed writing space in which to craft your ineffable fucking masterpiece. Maybe like me there are some days you get hives and feel like vomiting hot blood at the mere suggestion of setting foot in there. Or maybe you're scratching out your best work on the back of discarded junk-food napkins, living under a bridge and carrying a toothbrush shiv to protect your carefully hoarded stash of scavenged Vegemite scrolls from the other bums. Sorry, poets! I meant the other poets.

Whatever. Some days a change is as good as a ridiculously large advance check from a publisher with a drinking problem. Just as we can train ourselves into productivity, we can also train ourselves into sloth, desolation, madness and despair. If you've been turning up at your desk, cafe table, library nook or upturned milk crate under the highway overpass for a week and the inspiration is just not coming, maybe it's time to try something as simple as a change in scenery. From the desk to the cafe table, or from the library nook to that nicely ventilated highway overpass. You might find that just moving your writing space is enough to unblock the logjam in your head space.

Listen to Hilary Mantel:

> If you get stuck, get away from your desk. Take a walk, take a bath, go to sleep, make a pie, draw, listen to music, meditate, exercise; whatever you do, don't just stick there scowling at the problem.

> But don't make telephone calls or go to a party;
> if you do, other people's words will pour in where
> your lost words should be. Open a gap for them,
> create a space. Be patient.

Neil Gaiman suggests giving up for a couple of days. Just put the story away. Gaiman usually prints his out when he goes back to it. The change in format can be enough to shake a few things free. 'Start at the beginning. Scribble on the manuscript as you go if you see anything you want to change. And often, when you get to the end you'll be both enthusiastic about it and know what the next few words are. And you do it all one word at a time.'

This is good advice if you've got one of those little blocks, where the next line is like a delicious piece of bacon stuck between your teeth that you ... just ... can't ... get ... to. But sometimes, whole fucking wildebeest get jammed in there.

If wandering off doesn't help, try for a change within the story. If a scene isn't working, try writing it from the point of view of another character, even if you're writing a first-person narrative with only one point of view.

SWITCHING POINT OF VIEW

I had to do this in *Emergence*, the first of my Dave Hooper novels. Apart from Guyuk and Threshy, everybody's favourite trash-talking demons, Dave is the only narrator of that series. That's cool when he's on a roll, but I'd never written a book like that before and I found it difficult, sometimes impossible, to understand what the other characters were thinking. I often had no idea what they might do from one page to the next. Because I wasn't writing any scenes from their points of view, I just couldn't get inside their heads. It never developed into a full-blown case of writer's block, but it did slow me the hell up for a couple of weeks. The solution was to rewrite a couple of chapters from the POV of the characters other than Dave. This got me moving again and, for bonus points, gave me enough material to later publish an ebook, *A Protocol for Monsters*. Turns out different characters will tell completely different stories, even when they're about the same thing.

If you're not up for that, or you don't think it would help, rather than switching characters, switch scenes. Jump ahead a couple of chapters. Write that big fight scene you've been looking forward to, or the car chase, or, hell, I don't know, the beautifully realised internal monologue which resolves all of your principal character's seething contradictions, whatever. Just get out of the slough of despond you've been wallowing around in for three weeks.

If you want to go nuclear on the problem, switch out

the project itself. Go write something else. A blog post.
A long erotic letter to Senator Eric Abetz. He probably
doesn't get nearly enough of those. Just write something,
anything. You have to get the great, rusted iron wheel
turning again.

You have kick self-doubt in the dick.

KICK
SELF-DOUBT
IN THE DICK

A would-be writer friend once asked me about self-doubt – the internal editor whose blue pencil strikes through just about everything you write. You know this buzz-killing motherfucker. He stalked you through every tortuous minute of the three exquisitely painful years it took to scratch out the opening lines of your sure-to-be-Nobel-winning opus about the sad little village at the foot of the mountain where it rained all the time and nobody had enough to eat.

'The only way you can write the truth is to assume that what you set down will never be read. Not by any other person, and not even by yourself at some later date. Otherwise you begin excusing yourself. You must see the writing as emerging like a long scroll of ink from the index finger of your right hand; you must see your left hand erasing it.' – Margaret Atwood

Or, you know, maybe your internal editor is the sort who jumps up on the cafe table where you've been stealing wi-fi and drinking other people's leftovers and *oh-god-no* your internal editor is wearing no pants and *oh-sweet-Jesus* he's turkey-slapping you with those huge and hideously deformed genitals of his while you're still doing lines of cheap trucker speed and hammering away at your epic NaNoWriMo project, your balls out, bug-eyed crazy bangsplosion splatterfest mashing up all the best bits of *Sharknado* with that Korean web comic you read about a hurricane which catches fire but none of it matters because now you doubt yourself and you wonder if it was such a great idea to write that opening scene with the tsunami made of killer bees and you keep deleting and rewriting and deleting and rewriting and now you're way behind deadline and those genitals, those horrible engorged genitals, are right up in your face and you can't even think because the giant quivering Phallus of Doubt has you in its thrall and …

Well, you're not really making much progress, are you?

How do you stop second-guessing yourself? How, for instance, do you still the voice that whispers that your brave decision to eschew commas, periods, capitalisation, paragraph breaks, indeed any sort of formatting, in your devastating masterwork about the sad little village, was perhaps not such a great idea. Even though when you had it you knew it was a fucking brilliant idea, bro. The crushing weight of tectonic slabs of text would perfectly recreate the oppressive feeling of life for the residents of the sad little village at the foot of the mountain where it rained all the time and nobody had enough to eat. Readers would totally *want* to suffer through it because your beautifully realised – if relentlessly miserable – characters had to suffer through their lives on the unformatted page and the eerie consonance of their imagined experience with the lived experience of the poor bastards who bought your novel and tried to read it would be like some sort of nuclear-powered enlightenment thing. I mean, sweet suffering Christ, those pussies at the Booker and the Pulitzer and the Nobel should just admit defeat and cut you a fucking oversized novelty cheque right now.

Unless, of course, your creeping fear that maybe you're writing shit and should just stop right now actually does stop you.

Whispers *Because you probably are, you know. Writing shit, I mean.*

See! Right there! That's what the Phallus of Doubt sounds like in your ear.

So how do you ignore it? How do you keep writing?

Here's your pro tip. Here's what you paid for.

You say, 'Fuck that, dawg! Who cares what that stupid talking dick says?'

You committed to writing this sucker, you to need to lay those words down. Even a bad writer who wrote a bad book is an infinitely better writer than some fucking piker who talked a big game and didn't deliver so much as a shitty first draft. And my friend, they are *all* shitty first drafts. So when the Phallus of Doubt gets in your ear and starts spitting sweet treacherous nothings in there, you would – were you a hard-bitten professional writer – cockpunch that loser.

'So much of writing a first draft feels like running a marathon while drunk – you're just galumphing about, yelling and laughing and crying and praying to Sweet Saint Fuck that the end is near. And then at the end you collapse in a puddle of your own liquorsweats.' – Chuck Wendig

---

It's your first draft.

A draft. Get it? Nobody else has to see it, not even your real editor.

Some shockers from my own first drafts? Using the phrase 'non-male Americans' instead of 'American women'. Or a personal fave, 'the human wave surged towards him like a surging human wave'.

A first draft is your dirty little secret. It can be as woeful, as horrible, as embarrassing as you want to make it. Nobody ever has to know. Just you and the giant talking dick in your ear. And what the hell, you already punched his fucking lights out, so sit down, shut up and finish your damn book. I really want to know what happens with that tsunami of killer bees. (The one about the sad little village, I'll ... er ... I'll read that some other time.)

Later on, in the second, the third, the hundred and twenty-ninth drafts, that's when you let your real editor run free with her diabolical blue pencil. That's where you can legitimately spend hours, sometimes days, and in the worst cases years, worrying over what you've written. Is it good enough, should I change it, should I just give up and walk away?

Save all that neurotic self-loathing shit for the second draft at least. After you've had a break from the text. You'll be a lot more objective about what needs to go and what can stay.

'The second draft is a major shift, though. You're no longer in that period of unfettered creation. You now have to pick through the wreckage of your first narrative and find what's salvageable. (Really, the first draft is all barf and LEGO bricks. The second draft is picking those LEGO bricks out of the barf. Also, pro tip: don't eat LEGO bricks.)' – Chuck Wendig

---

And that's also when you can finally listen to the soft, rasping voice that comes out of the dark in the dead of night and scares the living shit of you because dead of night! Who the fuck is out there?

Oh, it's the Phallus of Doubt, and it really needs to talk about that 230 000-word sentence you wrote about the sad little village. Then, and only then should you sit back and sigh, 'Okay, you're a dick, but I'll listen. What about it?'

WORK ON MULTIPLE DEADLINES

Whether you're a grizzled old hack or a baby writer with one blog post to her name, you will quickly end up juggling multiple deadlines. That's cool, there's nothing special about it. Normal people do this all the time. High school students probably have more demanding deadline schedules than you. After all, you're a writer. I'm willing to bet that at three o'clock in the afternoon you probably haven't got out of your pyjamas yet.

Not judging, just saying.

'Deadlines refine the mind. They remove variables like exotic materials and processes that take too long. The closer the deadline, the more likely you'll start thinking waaay outside the box.' – Adam Savage

You might remember from high school what a train wreck felt like as all of those assignments piled up on top of you. In writer life, it's even worse because if you don't hand the assignment in, you don't get paid. Be nice if we could all follow Henry Miller's advice to 'Work on one thing at a time until finished' but we don't all have the luxury of living off our girlfriend's sugar daddy while we dawdle over the first draft of *Lovely Lesbians, Crazy Cock*. (Seriously, look it up.)

It doesn't matter if the most important thing in your life at the moment is finishing that PhD thesis, submitting the first draft of your difficult second novel, or nailing your daring reinterpretation of *Lovely Lesbians, Crazy Cock* as an epic libretto for Andrew Lloyd Webber's production company. You're probably going to have some other stuff on as well. Here are seven helpful hints for not fucking everything up.

1. Make a list. Put everything on there. Don't bother breaking it down into all the little baby steps you need to take to get to the end of your various projects. If Andrew Lloyd Webber is screaming at you for finished copy just write down, 'Lesbian

thingy!' If your dissertation is due next week and you haven't even started, you don't need to write down a step-by-step plan for breaking into the university library late at night, stealing copies of obscure English-language South American academic journals that nobody will be able to find on the internet, scanning the relevant articles and cutting and pasting them together into a perfectly plagiarised Frankenthesis. For now, just note down, 'Thesis'. Be expansive only in leaving nothing off the list. Everything goes on there. Your planned blog post about the 63 reasons Disney got it wrong by hiring JJ Abrams to reboot the *Star Wars* franchise when you were available to do the job at half the price? Check. Your mass mail-out to 300 literary agents inviting them to cage-wrestle each other for the right to represent you when Marvel inevitably buys the rights to *Lovely Lesbians, Crazy Cock* to kickstart its latest and edgiest superhero franchise? Check. Get it all on there. Use a pen and paper. The old ways are the best. Feel that organic connection between you and your destiny.

Have you done that? Are we good now?

Excellent.

2. Scrunch that fucker up tight, light it on fire and throw it at the television the next time you see an advert for *The Bolt Report*.

3. Prioritise. Make another list. This time you can only have three items on it, because even if you're a full-time writer, or student, or a committed layabout, getting three things done in one day is the limit of human achievement. You're fooling yourself if you try to do any more than that. And if you are not a full-time layabout, like me, if you only have an hour or so each day or every couple of days to devote to your writing, your list can only be one item long. Sorry, but that's the hard truth. Henry Miller was right. Pick one project and hammer it flat before you move onto the next one. If you are in the happy position of having whole days stretching ahead of you, tough shit again. You still have to choose that one project to get the lion's share of your attention, and one side project you can devote a little bit of time to after you have made your word count for the day. How do you choose the most important project? That's up to you. But a good question to ask yourself when making that decision is, 'Will this change my life five years from now?' If the answer is no, that's your side project.

4. Maintain your focus. We've already discussed this at length in 'How to avoid distraction'. There are some people who write like scary unstoppable Terminators. They can't be bargained with. They can't be reasoned with. They don't feel pity, or remorse, or fear. And they absolutely will not stop, ever,

until you are dead. Oh, no, wait. That's editors. No-body writes like that. Multi-tasking is bullshit and expecting that you can write like a machine is just as bad. If you have unlimited time to spend writing, give yourself a maximum of three or four hours a day. After that, you're fried.

5. Set your routine. Thought you might scribble a few lines out over coffee and madeleines at Cafe Proust today? Perhaps a surf and solid hour or so on the laptop under palm trees at the beach tomorrow afternoon? Or maybe you'd prefer to take this antipsychotic medication and nail your feet to the ground to stop yourself floating away on a cloud of LSD-flavoured wishes and dreams. Professionals turn up, every day, at the same time and they get the motherfucker done. If your peak creative writing time is five in the morning, you turn up then and you kick the arse of your primary writing project like a Spartan king. If you like a nap after two, you kick that nap in the arse and you scream, 'THIS IS SPARTA. ONLY THE DEAD SLEEP HERE', and you spend your slightly less productive time of day on a secondary project, like filling in this quarter's BAS form for the tax office. Then you Groundhog Day that big writing project until it's done.

6. Watch the horizon. While you've got your head down every day, slaughtering deadlines like a

Spartan champ, take half an hour once a week to look up and see what's coming at you as you do your bloody work in front of the Hot Gates. The days are long, but the years are short. This year, for instance, my to-do list features two long-form novels, heaps of ebooks, about 150 newspaper columns, and a bit of faffing around every day at my personal blog. Oh, yeah, and this fucking thing. That's a long to-do list. The exact opposite of what I told you to do when you are making up your list. But I won't work on all of those things every day. My best writing hours go towards one project. Another hour a day, I like to waste on my blog. Two things a day, every day, and only one of them really counts. Once a week I look towards the horizon and see what's coming at me so I can decide what deadline gets its arse kicked next.

7. Use the right tools. You don't need to invest elephant bucks in project-management software to juggle multiple deadlines. But you can't do it with just a word processor. Word processors aren't even that good at dealing with one deadline. Once a project gets to be longer than a few thousand words and you break it up over multiple files, the linear hierarchies of most word-processor file-management systems are pants. If you're going to be a professional, act like it. Bring the right tools (and check out my guide to writing apps in 'Use

the technology'). Some shit is unavoidable. There is an elegant sufficiency of word processors to choose from, for example, and we all hate Microsoft Word. But Word is unavoidable. When you submit a manuscript, that's what publishers want to see. An MS Word file, pages numbered, double spaced, Times New Roman, 12 point. Just grit your teeth and give Bill Gates his reach around.

8. Keep a notebook. Not an electronic notebook either. A real one. Like real writers use. There's a whole chapter to write about the benefits of always having a notebook with you; a whole book if you want to snag a copy of William Power's excellent *Hamlet's BlackBerry*. But when dealing with multiple deadlines and competing projects, nothing beats a notepad and pen for keeping your unruly, half-arsed Persian bazaar of a mind in good order. Carry one with you always. Devote different parts of the book to your different projects. And as crazy, unbidden inspiration comes upon you, as it will, don't lose focus on your main game. Quickly take up your notepad, jot down whatever just occurred to you, then put the motherfucker away with extreme prejudice. You can come back to it later, when you've finished your real work for the day.

USE THE TECHNOLOGY

Many writers suffer from repetitive strain injuries. It's an occupational hazard and it can be devastating. Some writers break their arms sparring with Muay Thai fighters because they foolishly attempted a stopping block rather than the more technically correct and less arm-breaky deflection block. Some writers who do this have 160 000-word manuscripts to edit the next day.

Okay, that was me. The night before I was due to start my second draft of *After America* I was training at a jujitsu class when I busted my arm. I threw out a lazy block, didn't move my body off the line of the attack, and heard my forearm snap like a dry twig when the kick slammed into it. I tried to tell myself it wasn't broken, because I had that manuscript to edit. I kept telling myself that as I drove myself home, one-handed. When my wife asked if I felt okay because all the blood had drained from my face and my arm was all swollen and misshapen, I muttered something about bruising it on the mat before washing down a couple of Nurofen tablets with a schooner of whiskey. Then I had a little lie-down.

My face-facts moment arrived at 2.15 in the morning when I rolled onto my broken limb. I was in surgery a day later having titanium plates bolted onto my broken bones. I arrived home from hospital to contemplate the impossibility of editing a manuscript when I couldn't put my hand on a keyboard or even pick up a pen.

This is how I know all about dictation software, just one of the many Borg-like augmentations I've made to my personal man-machine interface over the years. Dictation software is the tech I get asked about more often than any other, though, so we'll start there.

I busted my wing about seven or eight years ago, but I'm still using a speech recognition program to do a lot of my writing. That should answer the question I get online all the time. Is this stuff any good? Long story short, yes, yes it is. At least for certain things.

A warning. My first impressions of dictation software were influenced by the fact that I was kinda desperate for it to work. I literally couldn't type. I broke my left arm and I'm left-handed, so scratching out notes with a pen wasn't an option. Even pecking out a short email to my editor, Joel Naoum, explaining what had happened was a pain. Ripping out tens of thousands of words of new manuscript or editing hundreds of thousands of words of *After America* by hand were out of the question. If the technology didn't work, I was pretty much fucked.

The program I used was called MacSpeech Dictate, a new port of a venerable Windows-based package that was then and still is superior to the Apple-flavoured version. I say that as a guy who won't have Windows in the house. In this case, with this program if you're rockin' Satan's Own Operating System, you are in luck. Windows totally owns this space.

But I am using the latest Mac version of Dragon Dictate to compose this chapter and it's awesome enough for me. You have three or four options really if you want to use dictation software. You can buy the latest version of whatever product Nuance, the publishers of Dragon Dictate, have on the market, or you can use the software baked into the operating systems of the big three: Microsoft, Google's Chrome and Apple's Mac OS. Again it pains me to say this, but Apple's offering is the weakest of the three. It pains me even more to admit that Google's might be the best of the freebies simply because of the staggering amounts of data el Goog can feast on every day. Even so, it's not that great. If you're seriously looking at dictating big slabs of your work, you will have to seriously consider handing over some of the folding stuff for a dedicated app like Dragon. And as good as it is, there are caveats.

Nuance's program is an unusual product in that it really asks a lot of the user. If you're not willing to do the training, if you're not willing to understand the parameters of the software, and most importantly if you're not willing to read the fucking manual then forget it. It's not a cheap bit of kit and you'll do your dough cold. If you *are* willing to invest the time learning how to use Dragon and training the software to work with you, then it could be a incredibly powerful tool.

First question: does it really, *really* work? Seriously, JB?

Yes, and it's awesome. It is freakishly accurate, much more accurate than my own typing. And there is no need these days to speak in an American accent, stopping and starting in the style of the great character actor Mr William Shatner. (And yes, it does recognise the word 'Shatner'.)

But speech recognition is not *Star Trek*. It won't do everything out of the box. You *do* need to train it to listen to your voice, and the software needs to train *you* to speak to it. The more time you spend using Dragon, the more accurate it will become. But only if you take the time to update your profile.

Your profile is the software's understanding of how you speak, and to a lesser extent how you write. Think of it as a super-avatar. It also includes a lot of environmental information, so you might record one profile for dictating in a quiet room and a different profile for a noisy room. When you first start dictating, the program will make errors, and just as importantly you will make errors because you'll probably try to speak to it like a person, not just a bunch of code. If you mumble, cough, slur your speech, whatever, it will all be transcribed.

The first couple of days you'll spend a lot of time pointing and clicking in what's called the Recognition

Window. In this little box you'll find the program's interpretation of what you just said, and up to ten alternatives. Option number one is always Dragon's best guess but if option number six was the right choice you just click on that and it swaps out the copy. If none of the options were accurate you can choose one to edit and use that. After a couple of hours of doing this and saving your profile as you go, you'll notice a marked improvement in the program's ability to understand you. As you get more confident and you relax, you'll also find you're able to speak much more quickly and conversationally until you do get to that *Star Trek* moment where you just speak at the computer and the words magically appear on screen.

That's dictation, it's not editing. And editing is way more important than composition in determining whether your finished product is readable. When I broke my arm I had real fears that MacSpeech Dictate, the earlier version of Dragon Dictate, would be crap at editing, and it kind of was. If I simply opened up a huge manuscript and tried to edit the thing via voice command I would fail. There is just no way that telling a cursor where to go and what to do is anywhere near as efficient as using a mouse and keyboard. But you're in for a terrible hiding if you try to mix keyboard and voice commands. It just won't work, and you'll eventually crash the program.

It's all down to the cache. Dragon keeps two things in its mind: what you said and what it wrote. If you fuck up that delicate balance by using your mouse and keyboard instead of your voice you'll blow the cache apart and overwhelm the program.

That could be a deal-killer, because of the unwieldy nature of using voice command to edit. There is, however, a caveat. The software comes with its own notepad, a basic text editor in which you can compose your documents. The notepad, these days called DragonPad, is an exceptional environment into which to dictate. It is stable and robust and, most important of all, it allows you to edit with your mouse and keyboard. You can just place the cursor wherever you want, define whatever text you want, and dictate right over the top of it. The essence of editing.

This understanding was hard won.

Heed me on this, young Padawan.

I came to enlightenment after a couple of frustrating days of constantly crashing the system. It got to the point where I was so pissed off, so depressed and so fucking desperate that I went back and did what I should have done in the first place. I Read the Fucking Manual from start to fucking finish. The hottest takeaway was the importance of working within the program's notepad.

There is one final point I'll make about speech recognition. It *feels* weird. We become so used to 'thinking with the tips of our fingers' when we write that, the strangeness of talking to a computer can be too weird for some people to get over. You may find yourself thinking about thinking about dictating your writing and getting over that that might take a bit longer than simply mastering the mechanics of the software.

Is it worth the money? Would I recommend that someone who's never used dictation software run out and spend a couple of hundred dollars more buying it off the shelf?

I don't know. Remember that I had no choice but to use this software, so I was willing to put in a couple of weeks climbing a very steep learning curve. A lot of people just give up. But for me dictation software has been the axeman at the winter show, murderously hacking through the thick stump of many deadlines, chips and bark and hot sweat flying everywhere. That sounds kind of gross, yes, but sometimes you need to get through the work that quickly. And, yes sometimes you need to be the engraver, carving exquisitely small needlepoint details into a single line of text. There are other apps which can help with this.

CREATING A BUZZ

I'm not much impressed by those writers who 'work' in cafes. Or maybe I should say, I'm not much impressed by anyone pretending to be a writer – technical term: poet – who spends all of their days in cafes scribbling in notebooks.

Real writing means standing at your desk, pants down, screaming into dictation software. Headbutting and punching the screen may also be necessary.

But, according to science, there is something about the soft background hum of a cafe or anywhere really with a muted buzz, that somehow focuses the mind and increases productivity.

Don't question me. Science said so.

It might just be something to do with the lonesomeness of long-distance writing. You do go a bit shack-wacky after a while. Luckily, there's an app for that.

Noizio.

This thing sits on your desktop or fondleslab or batphone and pushes out the sound of a reasonably busy, but not chaotic cafe, bar or restaurant. It comes with different loops for different times of the day: breakfast, lunch and so on. It also offers waves, winter winds, gurgling streams, a campfire, a forest and more.

It seems completely naff and an utter waste of time, so of course I am addicted to it. With the right background tunes it is spookily like working in a cafe, but without the four-dollar flat whites.

Does it help? Really?

Honestly, I have no fucking idea. But it feels less lonesome than just throwing on music and hammering away at a manuscript. Give it a go. If you can stream ocean sounds from another device you could even have a beachside cafe.

I have four main programs I write in.

Dragon Dictate, which I've already discussed. Pages – which is my utility word processor, for throwing out columns, blogs, features and so on. I appreciate its elegance and simplicity, but Pages' file management system is arse with frostings of arse. As you generate more files, it becomes increasingly difficult to manage them by Apple's preferred method – tags. I still use Pages every day, but not so much for manuscript work. I'm not going to tell you what to use as your utility word processor. That really is a personal choice.

Anything longer than a column or short feature and I open up Scrivener – the crack cocaine of writer apps. It is purpose built for writers, by a writer who was so frustrated by trying to wrestle the unformed blob of a postgrad thesis and a novel into shape with a word processor that he decided to build a piece of software from the ground up; something designed specifically to help authors. There are whole books written about Scrivener. There are self-help groups devoted to its addicts. It's available for a free trial. Do yourself a favour and check it out. The document-management and structuring functions are first class. It is especially good at allowing me to keep a firm whip hand hovering over the structure of a long story arc. If you're looking for a writing app that gives you a God-like top-down view of your manuscript and granular scene-by-scene control, then this is your baby.

MS Word – what can I say? Every publishing house uses Word because every publishing house uses Word.

When it comes time to submit the draft, there is no avoiding it. This also means that redrafting and final edits are also done in Word, often on my iPad outside the house. I like to think the change of scenery freshens me up.

Other apps?

Besides Noizio I use Vitamin R for time tracking and management. It's like a nuclear-powered Pomodoro app and if I don't open it first thing in the morning I get a metric shit-tonne less writing done by the end of the day.

My research gets bundled into Evernote, before I shunt it across to Scrivener, but Evernote is starting to feel a bit bloated. You could like Microsoft's OneNote if you're starting from scratch. I use the Dictionary.com app on my iPad for its thesaurus (but a big ol' hardback copy of the Macquarie Dictionary for spelling and definitions).

For project management I used Cultured Code's Things 2 app. I'm not recommending it over OmniFocus or 2Do, but I will recommend you commit to your own task management software suite, especially if you have to juggle multiple commitments. All of these apps will help you wrestle with the unruly word demon lodged inside your head. Maybe the little fucker will even tap out. Maybe, you'll own that punk.

Maybe you'll write 10 000 words in one day.

WRITE 10 000 WORDS IN A DAY

Fear me, NaNoWriMo wimps, for your 50 000-word novel is but a brain fart to one such as I. You wrote your little booky-wooky in a month? And now you want a cracker? Bah! Take this stale biscuit of my disappointment and choke on it! You disgust me.

Real writers cough up 50 000-word novels with the black mucous of their toxic morning cough.

Every.

Fucking.

Day.

And you can too. Okay. Maybe not 50 large a day. I can't teach you how to do that. That's a secret thing we like to keep secret among the Hero League of International Superauthors and the other superauthors would get pissed if I gave it away. But yeah, you can totally write 10000 words a day. Not straight away, though. I need to ask a few questions first.

Can you type? Like really fucking fast? Because those 10000 words won't write themselves you know. It's gonna be your fingers flying across the keyboard in a kinetic blur of speed that will stress the very fabric of reality. If you can't type that fast, better learn how.

Or get that dictation software I was talking about.

Okay, so you've bought yourself a stand-alone dicta-tion rig.

Or you hit a Learn to Touch Type app really hard.

Or you paid cash in a Bangkok body-hacking shop for those Cyberdine Systems T-1000 wet-ware implants that turned you into a half-human, half-android ruthless killing machine of death with a verified typing speed of 1000 words per minute.

So now we're good to go. The physical limits which constrain puny humans are of no concern to us. We can type *reallyfuckingfast*.

Aaaaand … you're staring at a blank screen.

You got nothin'.

Ha! Foolish would-be writer. Did you imagine writ-ing fast was merely a matter of writing fast? Did you think your Cyberdine Systems wet-ware implants and bespoke speech-recognition software would do all the work for you?

Well, you were wrong.

Punching out massive daily word totals is not just a matter of typing fast or jabbering at a computer. There are many other arcane writer magics you must first learn. Turning off your modem is a good start. Chopping up your day with the Pomodoro method is another. Throwing yourself on the mercy of Rachel Aaron may be the most important.

Aaron is a keyboard-killing word ninja who went from dribbling out a couple of thousand words a day to spraying 10 000 words all over her manuscript every goddamned day while dealing with a newborn baby.

How the hell did she do that? It's her story, I'll let her start:

> I had a bit of a problem. I had a brand-new baby and my life (like every new mother's life) was constantly on the verge of shambles. I paid for a sitter four times a week so I could get some writing time, and I guarded these hours like a mama bear guards her cubs – with ferocity and hiker-mauling violence. To keep my schedule and make my deadlines, I needed to write four thousand words during each of these carefully arranged sessions. I thought this would be simple. After all, before I quit my job to write full time I'd been writing two thousand a day in the three hours before work.

> Surely with six hours of baby-free writing time, four
> thousand a day would be nothing...

Ha! Arrogant and foolish, like all new mothers. Her feeble plans came to nothing. Every day she would lock herself into the writing prison determined to make 4000 words. Every night she had to claw her way out of that prison cell with but a miserable 2000 words to show for her pathetic efforts. It was as though she had never quit her job or hired that babysitter.

'Needless to say', she says, 'I felt like a failure. Here I was, a professional writer with three books about to come out, and I couldn't even beat the writing I'd done before I went pro.'

Like all failures, she had her reasons, excuses and justifications. Her book *The Spirit War* was the hardest, most complex piece of writing she had ever undertaken. She was always tired because she could not sleep with a newborn in the house. The National Oceanic and Atmospheric Administration's latest research indicated a worrying acceleration in the thawing of the Russian tundra, raising the prospect that the entire system might reach a tipping point from which the planet could not pull back and which human civilisation could not hope to survive.

But in truth there were no excuses. Unless something changed she would not finish her manuscript and we would all die screaming in the violent maelstrom of climatic collapse.

Luckily she solved the more difficult problem first,

and almost by accident. Aaron, like most of us if we're being honest, wrote by the seat of her pants. She was what George RR Martin would call a gardener (see 'Wrestle your novel into shape'):

> This was how I had always written, it felt natural to me. But then one day I got mired in a real mess. I had spent three days knee deep in the same horrible scene. I was drastically behind on my word count, and I was facing the real possibility of missing my deadline ... again. It was the perfect storm of all my insecurities, the thought of letting people down mixed with the fear that I really didn't know what I was doing, that I wasn't a real writer at all, just an amateur pretending to be one. But as I got angrier and angrier with myself, I looked down at my novel and suddenly realized that I was being an absolute idiot. Here I was, desperate for time, floundering in a scene, and yet I was doing the hardest work of writing (figuring out exactly what needs to happen to move the scene forward in the most dramatic and exciting way) in the most time-consuming way possible (i.e., in the middle of the writing itself).

In that moment she became an architect. She closed up her laptop and got medieval on that story, taking out a pad of paper and a pencil and blocking out the scene in short, truncated bursts:

> I didn't describe anything, I didn't do transitions.
> I wasn't writing, I was simply noting down what I
> would write when the time came. It took me about
> five minutes and three pages of notebook paper to
> untangle my seemingly unfixable scene, the one
> that had just eaten three days of my life before I
> tried this new approach. Better still, after I'd worked
> everything out in shorthand I was able to dive back
> into the scene and finish it in record time.

She describes words flying onto the screen, and finding at the end of that session that she had written 3000 words rather than 2000, and most of them in that last mad dash at the end.

I had a similar experience moving from *Weapons of Choice* to *Designated Targets*. *Weapons* had taken me nearly three years to write, after I promised my publishers I'd finish in less than 12 months. Like Aaron I had my excuses. (That NOAA data is really worrying, you know.) But mostly I fucked up because I didn't know what I was doing or where I was going with that story. I just thought, *Lesbian fighter pilots with iPads kick Adolf Hitler's arse!* Give me my gigantic royalty cheque now, bitches!

With *Designated Targets* (Book 2 in the Axis of Time), and without having read Rachel Aaron's now famous blog post on how to crank 10 000 words a day, I decided to do something very similar to what she had done with *The Spirit War*. I blocked out each scene in much greater detail than, say: 'Hot lesbian + Maximum Nazi = epic arse kicking'.

I don't have the outlines for *Targets* anymore. But below is an example of the outline for a 3500-word chapter in *Stalin's Hammer: Cairo*, the second book in the Stalin's Hammer series which follows on from Axis of Time.

Julia's POV

al Nouri has stashed her in a Club Lounge guest room. Very swish. She can see the chaos on the green lawn downstairs.

No sign of Harry. His phone is dead. But hers has only one or two bars, intermittently.

al Nouri very pissed, but not at Harry. His people tell him 'the Jews' began firing.

'This is not how we do things.' He is very impressed that 'Your Harry, he executed the dogs'.

al Nouri is second cousin to some nephew of the King. He wants to send a message.

Julia's phone rings. Finally. It's Harry. Can't talk. All good. Coming back.

He is well pissed when he finds out what happened to Julia.

al Nouri wants to talk to him.

Harry agrees because the man saved her.

Can't talk on an open line.

Agree to meet in ten minutes. Come in through
servants entrance. Not staff. Servants.

The first thing this tells me, I'm writing this chapter
from Julia Duffy's point of view. She's a hard-knuckled
reporter with 31 flavours of PTSD. She's American. A
war correspondent. And she's shagging Prince Harry.
The chapters written in her voice are going to be very
different from those which Harry narrates. After that
we get into the scene-by-scene rundown. I didn't write
the whole chapter, but you can see the outline of it very
clearly.

Back when I blocked out *Designated Targets* I wasn't
looking to massively accelerate my daily word count.
I was just trying to avoid plunging into a death spiral
of writer's ennui by getting caught up in plot holes and
narrative dead ends. Working out what would happen in
each scene before it happened had that effect, but it also
stomped the pedal to the metal on my daily word count.

I'm not advocating a strict adherence to blueprints

here. Characters have to live and breathe and have their own adventures. In some ways you're just channelling what they have decided to do on the page. You can't force them to do something they don't want to do. Nor should you hold them back from taking a step that had not occurred to you. If a character wants to step through a door with a gun, let them. You might be surprised what they find on the other side. But if you make them step through a door with a gun, you better know damn well what's on the other side and what's about to happen when they find it. Raymond Chandler famously advised authors who'd written themselves into a corner to have a man with a gun come through the door. But Raymond Chandler so lost track of what was happening in *The Big Sleep* that when Howard Hawks, directing Humphrey Bogart in the 1946 screen adaptation, asked him in desperation who had murdered the chauffeur, Chandler admitted he had no fucking idea.

Does this mean you can plot out a whole novel before you write it? No, it doesn't and you can't. There are some problems in storytelling which can only be solved by the telling. But you don't write a book in one day. It's a long journey of many miles and taking a few minutes at the start of each day, or even a few moments at the start of each Pomodoro, to plan out or to simply ponder what happens next will get where you want to be that much quicker. Of Rachel Aaron's three suggestions, this is the most important.

She is a novelist and, like her, I'm explaining the

process as it applies to fiction writing, but knowing what you are going to write is even more important for non-fiction. Whether a 300-word blog post or a 6000-word feature for a glossy magazine which still has enough advertisers to pay you a dollar a word and cover all your expenses – they both need to be blocked out rigorously, even rigidly. A newspaper column of fewer than 600 words will normally contain one main idea. Over that length and you start to deal with increasing layers of complexity. At 1200 words, the standard length for a weekend news feature, you have a real bag full of snakes to straighten out. I'm telling you this from personal and painful experience, do not fucking wing it. Not only will you spend two or three times as long writing the damn thing, if you even make your deadline you're going to get slammed by rewrites when your editor gets a look at that piece of crap. Structure is everything in nonfiction, and you know who does structure really well? Architects.

Aaron's other two suggestions for massive word counts? Time and energy management. Having doubled her daily output by thinking about what she was going to write, rather than just planting arse to chair and letting rip, Aaron went looking for other ways to improve her productivity. You might have heard the phrase 'necessity is the mother of invention'. Here is a perfect example. She was still on deadline, she still had that newborn baby in the house, she was still racing against the thaw of the tundra. As many people discover, especially working mothers, the arrival home from the maternity ward of that ceaselessly mewling, shitting bundle of joy necessitates a few life changes. You quickly find you have no margin of error, no slack to call on and no fucks to give. You need to make this work.

Even if you don't have a newborn, if, for instance, you are trying to cram your writing in around full-time work commitments, you need to be as productive as possible in the few hours you actually get to write. Understanding how you go about the daily business of writing, what used to be called time and motion studies, would really help. But Rachel Aaron, again like most of us, had no fucking idea.

> I'd kept no records of my progress, I couldn't even tell you how long it took me to write any of my last three novels beyond broad guesstimations, celebratory blog posts, and vague memories of past word counts. It was like I started every book by throwing myself at the keyboard and praying for a novel to shoot out of my fingers before the deadline. And keep in mind this is my business. Can you imagine a bakery or a freelance designer working this way? Never tracking hours or keeping a record of how long it took me to actually produce the thing I was selling? Yeah, pretty stupid way to work.

Stat nerds will thrill to what happened next. Rachel Aaron collected data. Rachel Aaron made a spreadsheet.

And Rachel Aaron opened a can of whoopass on her productivity. The data points she collected? Time started; time finished; number of words written; and where she wrote. The patterns surprised her. She was most productive working in a coffee shop, probably because it had no wi-fi. She was most productive in the afternoon, not the morning, as she had assumed. And the longer she wrote, the faster she got. If she only had an hour, she might make 500 words. But if she had four hours she would burn through 6000 words, accelerating as she went.

She understood the rhythm of her working day and could plan to be more productive because of that understanding. You're not Rachel Aaron. You might want different data points, like how many words you wrote after eating three chocolate-and-banana muffins compared to doing three shots of wheatgrass juice. (Answer: nobody can do three shots of wheatgrass juice and live.) If you could be arsed studying your own workflow and rhythms you will get different results to Aaron, or me or to George RR Martin. But if you don't study them, you won't know and you will make poor decisions, like choosing wheatgrass over chocolate or writing *Game of Thrones* spin-off novels instead of delivering *The Winds of Winter* on time.

A personal example. *He Died with a Felafel in His Hand* was mostly written between 11 pm and 4 am over an insane five-week period. Looking back now I'm not sure why, probably because I was full of cheap red wine, amphetamines and bullshit. That experience queered my understanding of how I work and how I *should* work for years afterwards. I assumed I could just fart around during the day because I was a hard, two-fisted keyboard-punching motherfucker who could get all Hunter S Thompson on a manuscript in the hours before the sun came up.

Not so much, as it turned out. That undergraduate crap didn't even work in my undergrad years and it fucked me up completely in my 30s. I am ashamed to admit that I'm most productive in the morning. Chances are, you will be too. You'll only find out, however, by taking a cold-eyed look at yourself and how you work. Are you a night owl because that's how you're hooked up? Or do you start work at ten o'clock at night because you're a lazy, disorganised shithead? It might be a good idea to settle that question before you try to build a career on bad information. The upside of a couple of weeks of tedious data collection: knowing yourself, bringing your A-game to the writing table.

The last of Aaron's productivity tweaks, the one that got her up over 10 000 words a day, seems self-explanatory, even a little obvious. She calls it enthusiasm. I prefer 'energy'.

If you have ever surfed, you may be lucky enough to have caught the perfect wave, dialled yourself into the green room, with the turning of the world somehow reduced to the liquid crystal waveform wrapped around you. When you're there, nothing else matters. If you have ever achieved what psychologists call a 'flow state' with your writing, you'll recognise something similar. You're not even aware you are writing. The story is flowing through you and you're watching it happen. It's awesome. If only we could bottle that lightning.

But we can't.

We can try to capture something like the effect, though. When Aaron was poring over her spreadsheet she noticed that the days on which she torched her word count were those days when she wrote her favourite scenes, what she calls her 'candy bar scenes', the ones she'd been looking forward to. Get her a ticket to Stockholm, she has locked up the Nobel Prize for stating the fucking obvious, right?

Maybe not, because as she admits it raised a worrying issue. 'If I had scenes that were boring enough that I didn't want to write them, then there was no way in hell anyone would want to read them. This was my novel, after all. If I didn't love it, no-one would.'

She had stumbled, again by accident, on to the problem of waste paper. All those pages we grind out just to get to the good stuff. Do you think readers enjoy ploughing through that shit any more than we enjoy writing it? Not just no, but HELL NO! You don't want to serve up that tired old crap, so don't. When you're taking a few minutes to think about the scene before you write it, try to get yourself fired up, try to find the excitement, the hook that's going to pull the reader through this scene, through this chapter all the way through to the link at the end of the book that they hit like a drooling, half-moronic junkie because they need just one more sweet, sweet taste of whatever you're selling. Or, you know, if they're not reading an ebook, maybe they catch a bus to the bookstore or something.

'The pleasure is so important, it's the juice. It's the key to all of it. There's just nothing better than when a work gives off a sense of pleasure. It can be very serious or difficult work or tragic work, whatever, but there's a sense that fun was had in the making of it.' – Emily Perkins

---

If you can't find that excitement, they never will. You might have to change the scene, or ditch it completely. Getting rid of that dross will improve your book, but it will also speed up your writing time when you don't have to trudge through the swamp of something you don't really feel like writing. It's even more important with nonfiction. Web metrics have taught us that most people don't get past the first couple of paragraphs in a story. Web comments have taught us many don't even read past the title. That's as much our fault as theirs. Light the fire and set it to the page.

And that's it, that's how you write 10 000 words a day. Think about what you're going to do before you do it. Know yourself and how you write. Be ruthless and get fired up.

MAKING SOME BANK

DON'T WRITE FOR FREE, EXCEPT WHEN YOU HAVE TO WRITE FOR FREE

In 2012 Matt Smith was an aspiring freelance writer – that is, he was living under a bridge, dreaming of the day he could move into a real cardboard box. He's a podcaster now. (This commodious cardboard box is brought to you by Squarespace!) Joe Hildebrand was putting together the comment pages for *The Daily Telegraph*. Picture the affable Joe grinning and giggling as he plunges his arms up to the elbow into buckets of raw offal and tosses bleeding chunks into the gaping maw of a giant sharktopus with the head of Piers Akerman and the flat, dead eyes of Andrew Bolt.

Long story short, Smith, who was a part-time free-lancer with a reasonable track record of getting his byline into places like *Crikey*, *The Drum* and *The Punch*, had an idea for a quick piece about reality TV and the travails of the Ten Network. Hildebrand found it 'vaguely interesting' and offered to print it. (I've never before heard of an editor offering to print something they found only 'vaguely interesting', but if that's how they roll at *The Terror*, who am I to argue with success, or a giant hungry sharktopus?)

Smith was understandably excited at the 'commission'. (There's a reason for the air quotes, which I'll get to.) He'd never before submitted any copy to *The Terror*, which is far and away the most successful newspaper in Sydney. At least in terms of circulation, advertising and an unparalleled ability to spread gibbering fear and violent confusion among the lower orders. Hildebrand had asked him for a headshot to run with the piece, and Smith wrote back asking what dimensions he would require. He also, a little late in the piece as it turns out, asked about the word rate. The what now?

How much he would be paid?

Oh, how we laughed.

Hildebrand replied via email: 'Sadly we've got a moratorium on paid contributions at the moment mate, so I can only offer you fame. Any dimension headshot will do.'

Smith, somewhat taken aback, volleyed a return: 'Hi, Joe. That's a tough ask for an emerging/aspiring journalist – especially when sites like *Daily Life* manage to give contributors some money – so I hope you can understand my disappointment. Please run the Twitter handle at the end at least, and let me know when the piece will run. Photo attached.'

The photo would not be required. Hildebrand informed the would-be tabloid columnist that getting published in *The Terror* 'is a pretty massive deal for an aspiring journalist mate and you just blew it. Take your piece elsewhere.'

And that's it, the shareware-lite version. Writing for *Mumbrella*, Matt Smith made some reasonable points about the iniquity of successful tabloid newspapers expecting freelancers to work for … well, free, and you'll be damned grateful for the opportunity to do so. (An opportunity for free exposure that isn't offered to *The Terror*'s advertisers.)

Hildebrand points out that successful tabloid news-papers are inundated with unsolicited copy, contributor budgets are minuscule (he's not lying) and there are any number of other 'aspiring' writers who would be happy just to get that byline published. (Again, not lying.)

As a lifelong freelancer my sympathies were obviously with Smith. When a large commercial operation such as a newspaper accepts a piece for publication, they should pay for it. Even if the payment is only a token amount. Little fish are sweet, as Terry Lewis, the famously corrupt former police commissioner of Queensland once said. They may not feed you, but in the world of freelancing, especially when you're just starting out, those little fish do help convince the Tax Office that you're serious about running a business. Even a token payment allows a freelancer to begin claiming tax breaks on their costs. Ask Rupert Murdoch about the importance of tax breaks.

The equation begins to break down when you move into web publishing where the advertising revenue model is much more precarious and the precedent of free copy, aggregating and bottom feeding is now well established. A lot of what passes for news these days isn't. It's just scraped off the bottom of the internet. *The Daily Telegraph*, however, is not a bottom-feeding website.

On the other hand, I have some sympathy with Hildebrand or any editor who spends a significant proportion of their day dealing with entitled lackwits. (I don't include Smith among their number. He's a smart guy, looking to get on with business.) Anybody who has spent any time in publishing or media will have had the experience of clueless amateurs pressing upon them crumpled handfuls of poorly written notes, sometimes with diagrams, outlining some earthshaking story that needs to be published but can't be because the mainstream media is in the thrall of hidden powers and dark forces and yada yada yada.

And shit writing, of course. Editors see a lot of shit writing.

They also see a lot of hungry, hard-eyed young chancers, hundreds of them emerging from campus writing programs and communications degrees every year. All of them getting up in your face, ready to chew out your eyeballs if it moves them that little bit closer to their career goals.

So yeah, I can understand Hildebrand's snark and disgruntlement. But as a freelancer I just don't give a shit about it. His problems are not mine. Me and my people, we got our own problems.

So, let's get to the meat of this. What should Smith have done? In similar circumstances what should you do?

First of all, he should never have written the piece. And neither should you. At least not in the way that Matt Smith did: on spec, without even testing the ground before he stepped out. If you want to avoid wasting your time as a freelancer, do not go writing stories for editors who have not commissioned them.

Got a great idea? Or what you think is a great idea? Then you ring up somebody like Hildebrand, or email them, or DM them on Twitter, or whatever. And you pitch them the idea. Apparently, if it's even 'vaguely interesting' you're in with a shot at *The Terror*. But a pro tip from JB? Why don't you try and make it something more than 'vaguely interesting'.

If the idea is appealing to them and they agree to 'take a

look at it' – and that's all they will ever agree to – then you can ask them about the contributor budget. The word rate.

Your payday.

Prepare yourself for disappointment.

They didn't ask for your story. They don't need it. They might eventually want it. But unfortunately, Hildebrand is right. There are plenty of other writers and an almost unlimited supply of other stories going cheap, and in most cases free. And it's not just baby writers cutting the legs out from under the market. Politicians, lobbyists, academics, shameless self-promoters, urgers, pimps, front men, agents … They are legion, and they don't care about getting paid. They really do just want the exposure.

What do you do if someone like Hildebrand says there's no money in the kitty? Or that there is money, but it's a laughable amount, an insult?

That, my friend, is down to you. Personally, I just tell people to fuck off these days. Not always. I'll do a couple of worthy charity gigs every now and then. But mostly it's fuck off. This is how I pay my mortgage, feed my children, keep the hovercraft afloat, you know the sob story. The guy who turns up to fix the filter on my pool doesn't do it to 'get his name out there in front of people'. He does it for $140. Although, while we're here, Brisbane Pool Boys – I can't recommend them highly enough.

It might be that if you are in the position of a Matt Smith – you're a young, reasonably established but still 'aspiring' freelancer – you just swallow your pride and take the hit. Give them the copy. Add the published article to your portfolio. If your portfolio is looking pretty thin, especially for print-only material, a couple of pieces like that can help. But only a couple. You don't do yourself any favours by becoming known as someone who will give it away for free. If your copy is that good they will eventually have to pay you for it. I'd suggest a maximum of two or three freebies before you turn off the tap. If they're not paying you by then, they never will. They're just exploiting you.

How then to deal with an editor like Hildebrand who has told you the cupboard is bare, but he'd like to take your lousy, only vaguely interesting story anyway?

If you've decided to wear the humiliation, accept the power imbalance, and grab the marginal utility of getting your byline into hard copy, then don't be a dick about it. The cheeky fucker who's stealing your story is being a big enough dick for both of you. You don't need to come over like 'umble Uriah Heep, bowing and scraping and grateful for the chance to kiss their unwashed arse. But I wouldn't go showing them how much you've been hurt and offended by getting cornholed on payment either. Hard to believe, I know, but editors have feelings too, and mostly they're even more embarrassed than you are about the payment issue. You want to take it up with someone? The people who are really responsible for this? Get yourself a cheap flight to Google HQ and go kick down the doors of the boardroom.

Bottom line: there are occasions, very rare and mostly to be found in the earliest days of your writing career, when giving it away for free will work in your favour. But always remember you cannot make a living out of doing that forever, or even very often. If Joe Hildebrand doesn't have the money to pay for your article, perhaps Joe Hildebrand can do without it. I'm almost certain he'd agree.

COLLECT DEBTS

The hardest part of freelancing is not going out into the world on your own, no back-up, no support, no nothing. It's getting the goddamned money off the dick-weasels who sent you out there like that in the first place. It's a good idea to always have a dozen invoices stacked up for collection, because at least half of them will be to delinquent creditors. If you go down the writer's path, know that you'll also build up some useful skillsets that could lead to a bright future in the credit management industry, should your dreams of literary glory not work out.

A little personal history. Every autumn Nimbin hosts a harvest festival. The local farmers gather in the town to show off their best produce. Tourists travel up from Sydney and down from Brisbane to enjoy a week of celebrations and events, culminating in the harvest ball on the closing weekend. The farmers are not redneck National Party members, and the crop is not legal. Every April, Nimbin plays host to the dope harvest festival. It's awesome fun and if you can find the time you should tick it off your bucket list.

I was paid to go by a magazine called *The Independent Monthly*, sadly no longer with us, but if you've ever read Morry Schwartz's Melbourne-based glossy, *The Monthly*, you've seen a close analog, at least in design. Not so much in politics. *The Indy* was a quality production run in a businesslike fashion. I was paid a dollar a word to write a 3000-word piece about the dope harvest festival and all of my expenses were covered. This is why I became a writer, so that people would pay me thousands of dollars to travel around the country smoking dope. Believe in the dream, my friends. It could be yours.

I travelled to Nimbin with my mate Pete, who'd been commissioned by another magazine, *Juice*, to write 6000 words on the same topic. *Juice*, like *The Independent Monthly*, is no longer with us. Unlike *The Indy*, it was neither a quality production nor a well-run business. It was a music magazine (and not to be confused with *Juice Magazine*, which still covers the skate punk scene). Pete's expenses were not covered, and he had a hell of a fight in the end to get any money out of them. A fight I bought into.

We had a great time in Nimbin. Our press passes came with a giant spliff taped to them. Back in Sydney I filed my copy, presented my invoice and expenses, and was paid by the end of the week. Pete, not so much. After writing twice as many words for a fraction of the amount I was charging, he submitted his story and waited for publication. Most places won't pay you until the story is actually in print or available online.

A couple of months after we'd choofed our complimentary doobies, Pete called me from Brisbane. The story had been out for a while, but he hadn't been paid. He'd rung the office a couple of times chasing his money and he was starting to fear he'd never see it. The editor and accounts manager seemed to be in a lot of meetings. Every time he rang. The office communication system must have been a bit wobbly because they never returned his calls.

Luckily for Pete I lived nearby and would walk past *Juice* most days on my way to drop in on other, less delinquent magazines. I said I'd get his money for him, or as much of it as they'd hidden down the back of the couch. I knew there was no point going in and begging, no point appealing to their better nature. These guys were arse-clowns. Instead, I dressed in a pair of long pants, which I rarely do, and tucked a copy of the form guide under my arm, getting into character.

My character was Mr Jack Podesta, principal and owner of the Never Fail Debt Collection Agency. I rolled into the magazine's offices, past the protests of the girl on the front desk and into the panic room where the editor was hiding. He didn't know me because I knew all about these guys by now and refused to work for them. I was also less of a minor public figure at that point and so had anonymity on my side.

The editor, a reedy-looking college boy, flushed bright red when I introduced myself as 'Mr Podesta, principal and owner of the Never Fail Debt Collection Agency'.

The conversation which followed was surreal, and I have to confess to recalling it with shameful joy, lo, these many years later.

'I understand you owe my client, Mr McAllister, a significant sum of money. I have come to secure it for him.'

All of the high colour which had rushed into his cheeks suddenly disappeared, leaving him sallow and a little dizzy on his feet. He burbled something about cheque runs and invoicing schedules and bullshit this and smokescreen that. I leaned into his personal space and let him have a blast of bacon breath and growled, 'I'm not interested. He wants his money. Now.'

More jabbering followed about cashflow and creditors and the right way of doing things, and I pointed out that the right way of doing things usually involved paying your bills. There was a copy of the magazine on his desk, featuring Pete's article, as it happened. I picked it up and flipped through. It was full of adverts and I asked the editor whether he was running them for free. He wasn't, of course, but I knew I had him when he started babbling about having had 'no agreement' to pay Pete for his story.

'Strike me purple, son', I said, seriously – I was deeply

into this character. 'What sort of an operation you running here? You're telling me you get people to work for you and you have no agreement to pay them? That's an extraordinary business model, son. But I don't think it's legal.'

More babbling, more panic, more looming and glowering and the violation of personal space by Mr Jack Podesta of the Never Fail Debt Collection Agency followed, culminating in a suggestion that perhaps in lieu of payment I should probably just take a couple of computers and see what kind of price they might fetch on the second-hand market.

Pete had his money by three o'clock that afternoon.

This is what we call the personal approach, and as much fun as it can be, it's not recommended for everyone or every circumstance. It worked in this case because the people at the magazine didn't know me. I was just some ugly man who wandered in wearing an ugly shirt before ugly shirts became hip again. Mr Podesta did not appear to be someone who could be brushed off. When he suggested taking expensive and vital office equipment in place of a story fee, it seemed to be a genuine threat. The act would not have worked if anybody at the magazine had recognized me or if the editor had been into mixed martial arts or something.

In most situations where you are forced to chase money and suspect you might never see it, you're better off outsourcing the effort to the likes of the Never Fail Debt Collection Agency. Or an agent, or a union.

Not everybody needs an agent or can afford the percentage they rake off your income. Anyone primarily working in nonfiction, even long-form narrative nonfiction, should forget about agents. They do their best work negotiating book, movie and TV deals. Save them for that.

So let's say you've written your 6000-word piece on the Nimbin marijuana harvest and festival and you haven't been paid. Who you gonna call? The Media, Entertainment and Arts Alliance, that's who. This is the union representing journalists (and clowns). They live to shake down delinquent creditors on behalf of their freelance members.

Example? A long time ago in a galaxy far far away I was commissioned by the features editor at *Playboy* to write a couple of thousand words about the marijuana industry. (Look, I've already told you why I got into writing.) Unusually I wasn't working alone. *Playboy*, or rather the now-defunct Australian edition, commissioned four freelance writers to prepare four separate pieces which would all be tied together in a bumper issue relaunching the magazine as a trustworthy source of investigative journalism.

Pity the porno guys weren't a trustworthy source of income.

We did our research, hit the road, took photos, recorded interviews, dodged a few tight situations with the wallopers, and filed our copy. The issue came out. Everybody read it for the articles. And … nada.

Same old same old. After a couple of weeks of patiently waiting for the invoices to be paid we checked with each other and discovered nobody had seen a cent. The editor and features editor never seemed to be around to take our phone calls. The accounts manager had just 'stepped out for a moment'. You can guess how it went.

In those days, *Playboy*'s offices were just around the corner from where I lived in Darlinghurst. If you think this gave me an advantage in chasing my invoice, you don't know much about freelancing. I went in two or three times to remind them of their responsibilities, but without the magic persona of Mr Podesta to call upon, I was shit out of luck.

Or I would have been except that I was a union member. I knew that sooling the union onto *Playboy* would sever my relationship with them, but what the hell. Magazines, newspapers, websites, basically anybody who doesn't pay their bills is on the way out of business anyway. So I called the union, which was known as the Australian Journalists Association in those days, and they sent the hard boys around. Or made enquiries on the telephone, or something. Whatever. I had my money by the end of the week. The other three guys, who'd done just as much work? They ended up with one-tenth of one per cent of fuck all.

Membership of the Alliance isn't free. For a lot of you, struggling to get paid a fraction of a cent a word by scammy online publishers, it might not even be afford-able. But I guarantee you without it you are going to get ripped off. If you can find the quids from somewhere, you should join up.

GET YOUR ENTOURAGE

So, you've written the final line on your soon-to-be bestselling novel, perhaps a high-octane hyper-accelerated international super-thriller, perhaps a dense and unreadably brilliant inner-dialogue-driven character study of three generations of strong-willed women.

The first question I'd ask as you hurried through the shining black marble foyer of the international publishing house you have personally chosen to receive your heartbreaking work of staggering genius is, what the hell are you doing? Where is your agent? Or even your lawyer?

There is a difference. Agents get paid a percentage of your earnings, motivating them to pump up your income. Lawyers simply charge you for their time, often in hugely expensive six-minute increments. But they don't feed off everything you earn for ever after.

Lawyers understand contracts. Agents understand the industry. Lawyers, within reason, will take on any client who can pay. Agents can be as picky as publishers about who they let onto their books.

If you have only one project you want to publish, get a lawyer. If you're looking to build a career, try to find an agent. The media and publishing guides mentioned earlier all carry listings, and just like publishers and writers, agents tend to specialise. But whether they're into fantasy, or golf memoirs, or visually arresting how-to guides for plushy fetishists, one thing all agents should be able to do is get you past the slush pile.

Sure, we've all heard about publishers plucking a diamond from the slush pile of unsolicited manuscripts, but that Almost Never Happens. In fact, it's so rare that the exceptional, almost singular nature of such a unicorn moment is imbued with the power to blind would-be novelists to the brutal realities of their industry.

Write this down. Publishers hate unsolicited manuscripts. Yeah, they do sift through them, because they're no more inured to the magical fantasy of that one special find than are the legions of unpublished authors burying them under a mountain of mostly un-fucking-publishable manuscripts.

And you know who sifts through them? The resentful intern, that's who. The young achiever who's already burned their own manuscripts, hopes and dreams in sacrifice to Baal for an entry-level position in one of the worst paying 'professions' in the world. You really want this tweedy suck-tooth making the call on your future? Based on a 30-second scan of the first two pages of your dazzling manuscript?

Whispers 'Then get an agent, you fucking idiot.'

And yes, some special exceptions to the unsolicited manuscript rule do exist. Genre publishers, especially ebook-only genre publishers will actually call for submissions once a month, or even once a week. But just keep in mind, they are insane. So if you're writing in a specific area, say, romance or military science fiction, in which a digital-only genre publisher is trawling for talent, you might get lucky.

But if you really think you have something special in your bottom drawer, or nowadays on your data stick or cloud service, do yourself the favour of running it past the jaundiced eyes of one of the industry's foulest, most nihilistic misanthropes – an agent. With an agent in your corner, you don't even have to read chapters like this. With an agent, you merely concern yourself with banging out 500 or 600 pages of top-shelf word processing, and they do the rest; including the all-important task of making first contact with whichever publisher you plan on shaking down for an unconscionably large advance. (More on this happy shit later.)

Publishers deal with agents all the time, and although they don't necessarily like them, they do like what agents do – at least insofar as agents protect them from the shower of shit which pours into the slush pile, day and night. Granted, they don't much like agents when said agents ratchet up the size of that unconscionably large advance, but there has to be a price for everything, doesn't there?

One caveat. When choosing an agent, avoid any that charge you a fee for their services. The only time an agent should put a hand in your pocket is when they have made a sale and are taking a commission. Reading fees, edit fees, manuscript assessment fees, these are all recognised as the work of charlatans posing as agents. Editors do that sort of work and they legitimately charge for it. Agents don't.

There are editing and manuscript assessment agencies around, and some are totally worth the money they ask. Under certain circumstances, you'd be an idiot not to use them. But they are not agents. They do not sell your work.

So, let's say you don't listen to JB. Let's say you have inexplicably decided to do your own pimping and nego-tiating. Perhaps you don't fancy turning over somewhere between 10 and 20 per cent of your income to the mis-anthrope. Perhaps in your day job you eat high-priced negotiators for breakfast. Perhaps as a child you fell out of a tree and now have an undiagnosed brain injury. Yes, that sounds the most likely reason for not listening to JB. Let's go with that.

There is a difficult, preliminary question you need to ask yourself before you charge through the doors at Penguin Random House, stripping off your clothes pre-paratory to diving completely nude into the giant money

pit they keep topped up in the basement for their con-
tracted authors. It's a difficult question, because you're
not qualified to answer it.

As you hurry through that black marble foyer, tracked
by the invisible lasers and defence turrets of the Pan
Macmillan in-house security system, or the slaver-
ing attack dogs of Rupert Murdoch's HarperCollins,
perhaps you should ask yourself: 'Do I even need this
publisher?'

It's not the sort of question publishers like to encour-
age, but increasingly authors are asking themselves
the very same. Let's illustrate the point with a little
experiment. If you have web access handy, pop over to
Amazon, the world's largest online book retailer and
festering sink of evil, and do a subject search under
Kindle for, say, mystery and thrillers. There you'll find
some familiar names. Lee Child, Janet Evanovich and
so on. But who are all these people you've never heard
of? With titles that seem to cost 99 cents?

Well, they may not be the future of publishing, but
they will be part of it. Self-published authors who moved
swiftly into the ebook space while the slow, lumbering
engines of olde worlde publishing were still banking up
the coal supplies for their steam engines. There are now
any number of options for unsigned authors to say, 'The
hell with Random House, I'll publish myself'.

Some of them have made a pile of money. Some of
them because they are awesome. And some of them
because they were fast to market, they were cheap,

sometimes even free while they established their name as a micro-brand (see the later section 'Find your readers and make them pay'), and because they could often put half a dozen small ebooks into the channel while the publishing houses were still dunking their Tim Tams into the Earl Grey at monthly acquisitions meetings.

Even established authors are beginning to examine the prospect of going it alone. Or perhaps not entirely alone, but certainly without the help of a publisher who'll generously let you have a bee's dick of a royalty, as opposed to the whacking fat 70 per cent you can earn going freelance.

Of course, as a freelancer, you'd have to organise editing, production, placement, marketing if you intend to do any, and so on (see 'Publish yourself'). There are now any number of businesses providing these services. Some are reputable. Some are just retooled vanity publishers. You'll need to do your own research as to whom you've fallen in with. The Writer Beware website is a good place to start.

Let's hand-wave all these modern confusions and tergiversations aside, however, and proceed on the assumption that you are an old-school writer with an old-school proposition. (And a small amount of brain damage, because you think you can do trade publisher negotiations all on your lonesome.) You have a saleable manuscript and you would like to sell it directly to a publisher. What do you need to know?

Well, what are you selling?

It's not just your beautiful prose.

You are selling rights to commercially exploit that prose in any number of formats and markets. The publisher will want the rights to everything, up to and including your DNA. When they rush you with a contract, fountain pen and a hypodermic syringe, just take a moment to say, 'Whoa'. You may not want to assign a small Australian publisher the right to market your work in Romania or, possibly more importantly, in the US. You may want to withhold foreign rights, audio rights, video game rights and so on.

Try that on your own and watch as they laugh in your stupid face. They'll probably bitch-slap you for your arrogant naivety.

No, in fact they won't. They'll get the intern or the fucking work experience kid to bitch-slap you for your arrogance because you are such a silly bitch you came at them without an agent and you tried to eat their lunch.

An agent comes at them, a publisher knows that heavy mofo is packing three or four different sets of semi-automatic hardware under that long black coat. They know for a laydown certainty that very same stone-cold killer fucking *buried* poor Brian from YA and Children's fiction last month. The fact that no-one ever found the body proves it.

But no, you go ahead and do it yourself.

Because there are so many traps for young players I'm sure you'll be just fine. Let's say, for instance, you invent a whole story universe, filled with compelling creatures

and characters and worlds. You write a series of successful novels within this universe but then move on, only
returning to it years later. Suddenly, after announcing
you intend to return to your roots, a lawyer's letter
arrives informing you that said roots are owned, root
and branch, by the original publisher. You didn't just
sell them the words in the manuscript. You sold them
everything. The creatures, the characters, the entire
universe. The very fruits of your imagination.

This is why you should either have an agent or an IP
lawyer in your corner doing the talking. The power,
unfortunately, is mostly with the publisher. Negotiations
can be brutal. You're an artist, you don't do brutal. But
your misanthropic agent or lawyer was born that way.
Let them do their worst so you can be at your best.

They are the ones who will discuss the all-important
filthy lucre. Just how much are you expecting to trouser
for this deal? Better not be too much. Advances are falling across the industry as it restructures to deal with
the advent of electronic publishing (where the industry-
accepted advance for ebook-only deals is one-tenth of
one per cent of fuck-all; which is to say, zero). The virtual
collapse of the US economy in the Great Recession and
the subsequent contraction of its publishing industry is
also feeding through to the rest of the world, undermin-
ing confidence.

There is no reasonable, generally agreed figure you can
settle on for an advance. If you are a first-time author,
don't be surprised at the insulting, piss-poor amount

on offer. It's an advance. If your work is that brilliant it will sell a million copies and you'll be rolling in royalties with only the tax office goons to ruin your party. There are some authors who think making a publisher bet the house on a book is good business. Or rather, there are some ex-authors who think making a publisher bet the house on a book is good business. It's not. If they take a bath on your first book, no matter how much potential they see in you, you're not getting a second deal.

Having settled on who owns what, and how much dough is changing hands, it's time to think about the nuts and bolts of your agreement. Exactly what happens in the case of failure? Either you failing to deliver, or the publisher failing to get the book to market. Ideally, if they make a hash of everything, you need to be in a position to recover your rights to your work. Alternately, if you make an utter cock-up of things, how much are you going to have to pay them back? The full amount of the advance? With interest? Best to know. Used to be that in the days of gentlemen's agreements, advances were never recovered. Those days are over. Cross these motherfuckers now and they will send a team of former Stasi wetwork operators after you with instructions to make an example of your mutilated corpse. They'll probably leave it on your mum's front doorstep.

Let's assume, however, you do deliver and they publish. Will there be a marketing budget for your book? Will you tour? It's a sad reality that the sales of books increase in direct proportion to the amount of effort that goes into pimping them out. Be careful that you're not expected to organise and run your own publicity efforts. Unless marketing and publicity is your day job, you'll fail. Get the publisher to spell out exactly what they intend to do in this area, in print. Then watch them renege on the deal.

Remember that time I said, 'Be careful you're not expected to organise and run your own publicity efforts?'

Yeah, you're totally gonna be expected to do that and smile like a shit-eating rube while you do. After all, you've got a Twitter account, don't you? With 137 followers? And another 200 Facebook friends? There's your market, champ. Now get selling!

As sad as that scenario is, marketing and publicity budgets are always under pressure, and it's the mid list and the newbies getting squeezed the hardest.

Two words: don't panic.

We won't get into it now (see the later section 'Pimp your book'), but if publishers expect us to carry more of the promotional burden, and they do, there's no point whining about it. Build your own promotional machine and ride that bastard like a hog.

This is getting off topic, though. So let's drag ourselves back to the mainline: your stupidly dangerous and ill-informed decision to represent yourself instead of using an agent or paying a lawyer.

Did it occur to you that there may be costs associated with your work? For instance, will there be an index? Under no circumstances agree to pay for it. Professional indexing is hella expensive. So too with permissions for photography. As perverse as it might sound, even public institutions like libraries will try to charge you for access and publishing rights to material they hold (paid for by the taxes extorted from your good self before you foolishly gave up merchant banking for the composing of epic poems). If there is a production cost involved in bringing your work to print, don't be the one left holding the bill.

On a closely related matter, if you are really looking forward to defaming somebody, you might wish to secure an indemnity from your publisher. Best not to defame anyone in the first place, of course, but given the antediluvian nature of Australian libel laws, even the best of intentions can go pear-shaped. Ask Bob Ellis. Or better yet, don't. Just learn from his hilarious example (see the next section, 'Don't get sued').

Once these tedious issues are settled you can get to the very heart of the author–publisher relationship: power. In the end, whose book is this? Do you have final say over its content and form or do they? Again, be wary of coming on as an overweening tool. While you may have very strong ideas about, say, the cover design of your precious tome, it might be that in matters of print aesthetics you don't know your arse from a hole in the ground. (Agents are useful at this point too if your publisher's proposed cover seriously makes you want to vomit hot blood in their eyes, but you don't have a say on the matter. Let your agent deal with it.)

So too with editing. What makes you think that after three or four rewrites you have any capacity to objectively judge what needs to happen to your manuscript before it's released to the paying public, who, believe me, can very quickly morph into the baying public? By all means, lobby for final control, but try not to exercise it.

There are two last issues you need to keep in mind. Publishers get very jealous of their authors. When they say they don't want you releasing 'competing' titles, they mean it. Sometimes, in the real world, delays and changes of allegiance can mean you have an older title with a previous publisher coming out at or near the same time as your new book. It should be possible to deal with such instances like grown-ups.

But publishers are increasingly on the look-out for authors going rogue – releasing, say, a self-published ebook of short stories or magazine columns at the same time as the publisher's title. They hate this, in the general and in the particular. Contracts have been voided because of it. They're idiots, because they're working off a zero-sum gaming model that might have applied in the olden days when they released about six books a year, but suck it up. You decided to work with them for the privilege of seeing three copies of your little booky-wooky misfiled on the wrong shelves at the back of Dymocks, so you have to play the zero-sum game now.

Which brings us at last to a final consideration. What happens at the end? Chances are you won't be with this publisher unto the grave. When the link is sundered what happens to all those rights you gave them when things were fresh and the very air itself was humming with mutual love and admiration?

At the very least the rights should revert to you when the book goes out of print. Traditionally that meant your title was dead. It was an ex-parrot. There was nothing in it for them or presumably you. But of course that was in days before print on demand, or self-publishing. I recently contacted a former publisher to enquire about the rights to an ex-parrot I was thinking of bringing back to life, as a self-published ebook.

I stupidly made the call myself.

I should have sent my killers.

But I didn't.

I could hear the slow toxic spread of the empty smile across her face as the publisher's intern said, 'Oh, no. It might not be in print, but is available print on demand. As if anybody would ever fucking bother, MWUHAHAHAHAHAHAHA.'

And then the intern bitch-slapped me.

Next time, I'm sending my killers.

Meantime, perhaps you really should get that agent. Or a lawyer. Nobody would normally want to hang around with a lawyer. But the minute you get sued, you're gonna want their hot tongue all over you.

DON'T GET SUED

Even neo-Nazis have rights. And lawyers. I learned this to my cost many years ago working on a story for *Rolling Stone*. I spent a couple of months investigating the neo-Nazi movement in Sydney. It wasn't huge. It wasn't networked the way these groups are now. It was mostly just a bunch of sad, fat blokes without girlfriends who liked to stand over Asian people before it became more fashionable to stand over Muslims. What sort of evil arseclowns were these guys? One of them was murdered in their own clubhouse, shot to death. He was wearing a T-shirt that read, 'Say no to gun control laws'.

I wrote two versions of this story for *Rolling Stone*. The first one, which named names, levelled accusations and pretty much charged into the narrative like a runaway petrol tanker into a tea party on the front lawn of an old people's home, would have got us sued. More importantly, it would also have resulted in a mistrial for at least one of the shitheads I was writing about, and probably for a couple of his shithead minions. The public good was better served by these guys going to jail than by me getting a really kicking story into the mag. So I pulled the names, changed the deets and dialled everything back to a place where the lawyers wouldn't come calling.

Or at least, I thought I had.

In the course of researching the story I'd met a source who was able to provide some very useful background information. My source also provided a great photograph of a dozen or so men in a motley collection of army surplus camo gear – extra large, to hide the murder boners they were all getting from being such bad-asses – and strangely futuristic-looking weapons which turned out to be paintball guns. They had been training for White Revolution by running around the scrub with toy guns and lots of bright primary colours.

It was a great image and it ran in the magazine.

Thing is, I sort of expected the editors to blur out the faces. My source assured me that what we had here was a collection of fair dinkum Neo-Fascists, but without seeing signed copies of the membership forms of the Nazi Party and a stamped receipt for their membership dues, who the hell was I to be calling them Nazis?

Here is a lesson for you. The story you most want to believe is the story of which you should be most sceptical.

Also, don't expect your editors to do everything for you.

Turned out one of these guys was not a neo-Nazi. He just liked hanging around with them. Thousands of dollars and a grovelling apology later, lesson learned.

It's tempting in the era of the internet, when you can publish anything everywhere instantly, to do just that. But as a growing number of bloggers, Facebookers and Tweetenvolk can attest, obscurity is no defence when the defamation lawyers come calling. You might not be writing for a national magazine. Your widely unread little blog may not have an actual audience beyond el Goog's creepy fucking internet spiders, but you can still be sued. And chances are you will lose.

Know this about Australian defamation law: it was crafted to protect the interests of 18th- and 19th-century gentleman hypocrites, and it has adapted very well to the 21st century. Have you ever met a defamation lawyer wrestling with an underfed poet late on a Sunday afternoon, just to claim that last two-dollar packet of Generic Budget Mince at the supermarket? No, you haven't. Because on Sunday afternoons your average libel lawyer is lounging around in his mansion, stretched out in his designer recliner, gently drumming greasy fingers on the grossly distended skin of his belly, contemplating the very fine lunch of *sous-vide* baby harp seal he washed down with a rather passable glass of the '47 *Cheval Blanc*.

The poet meanwhile is stuffing ground-up raw offal into his face and wondering how a simple limerick about a crooked politician that nobody even read on his stupid WordPress blog could have brought him to this pass.

Does this mean you can't write nasty things about people who really, really deserve it? Hells bells no!

If somebody does something or says something which offends you, you can say the most appalling things about their argument, and to a lesser extent about their behaviour, just as long as you don't give their barrister a chance to argue that you have impugned their actual character.

Example?

Some years ago the trollumnist Mr Andrew Bolt assayed an argument that the prime minister of the day, Ms Julia Gillard, had blood on her hands because her government's asylum-seeker policy was directly responsible for an increase in people smuggling, and therefore responsible for any deaths at sea resulting from that smuggling. The point is arguable from both sides, but Mr Bolt is not much concerned with rarefied discourse, and the creeping, if not sentient slime mould which lives in the comment threads beneath his blog posts, not at all.

How then to respond? I do not know Mr Bolt personally, but I'm sure he is a fine fellow of unimpeachable personal standards. It would be wrong of me, as well as legally fraught, to imply anything else. Mr Bolt's arguments, however? Ah, his arguments are a different matter. His arguments do not have a reputation. They cannot retain a QC. His arguments are not him, and they can be assailed with impunity. The pars below are copied from a column which was published nearly a day late because every word was checked by lawyers and most of them changed before publication.

> Confronted on *Lateline*, by David Marr, about Howard's history of playing fast and loose with the truth during the 'Children Overboard' scandal, and whether it weakened his case for war, Bolt retorted, 'What is possibly the advice that you think he has that you don't have access to that could change your mind on this? Because, really, I see no claim that he makes that cannot be utterly substantiated by material that's right on the public record, that you can see for yourself if you bother to check.'

> And thus hundreds of thousands of Iraqis were utterly substantiated to death, their country laid to waste and condemned to a perdition of blood and savagery. Not to worry though. I am sure their deaths were liberating and any ruin and destruction was a merciful release from the tyrant Saddam's bane.

> Of course, should any of them lack a taste for slaughter – perhaps because they stood so much closer to it than courageous Bolt – should they attempt to flee the carnage with their children in

small, overcrowded boats, for instance ... then damn their eyes! They are jumping the queue. They are assailing our precious sovereignty. They might very well be terrorists! Send the navy and turn them back. Turn them back. Turn them back and if they founder and are lost then whose fault was that? Certainly not ours.

Boiled down to essences, his arguments, rather than his character, are brought under fire, in this instance through the technique of framing the rhetoric as if to agree with them and even amplifying their stupid, unthinking brutality. The sentence 'I am sure their deaths were liberating and any ruin and destruction was a merciful release from the tyrant Saddam's bane' is on the face of it ridiculous, but it is merely the logical end point of that line of argument. The same technique as applied in the next paragraph, with the volume turned up to 11. Note that nowhere is it stated that Bolt himself has said this. The column does not contend with the man, only with his rhetoric.

I had the benefit of highly paid lawyers to check and change my copy, of course. You do not. How then to avoid losing your house, or your favourite cardboard box under the bridge if you are a poet?

Stick with the basics.

If you are asserting a fact that will damage the reputation of an individual or a company, you'd better be able to swear under oath that you did your due diligence in researching that fact. In old-school journalism the standard was to check a contentious fact with three independent sources. Is that a pain in the arse? You bet. But not as much as losing a defamation case.

Those sources, by the way, need to have direct knowledge and/or evidence of whatever villainy you are alleging. 'I heard three separate guys on the internet say this! Three of them!' is not a defence.

And don't get all cocky if you think none of this applies to you because you don't do investigative journalism. Australian literary history has a couple of examples of novels which came under fire because a character or characters in them too closely resembled some thin-skinned villain in the real world. Of course if I name them, the villains – were they alive – could come after me for a second helping of defamation dessert, simply because I had implied they were a villain.

Is there some magic wand you can wave over your writing to protect it from the dark arts of the libel lawyer? Not really. If you are an eager young satirist just dying to share that hilarious idea you had about Chris Kenny and a dog, you could just not. Perhaps by cutting that joke, you might be forced to come up with something funnier?

If you are a restaurant critic you could avoid using metaphor to describe a really ordinary meal.

'Really, Mr Schofield? Have you ever actually eaten an old leather boot? Would you care to show the court how one might do such a thing, since you claim to have had a very similar experience in my client's restaurant?'

If you are Bob Ellis you could avoid printing rumours about the wives of prominent Liberal politicians as though they were established facts, and/or entertaining all three readers of your blog with those allegations about me that would have nicely funded an extension to the back of my very large house. (Unfortunately that post has been deleted, possibly by Bob's lawyer or long-suffering wife, and so my dedicated disco lounge remains unfinished.)

Bottom line? Take care, check your facts, don't let your outrage get the better of you.

Remember, you live in Australia. We don't have a First Amendment. We just have lots of lawyers hungry for delicious baby harp seal.

PUBLISH YOURSELF

Remember when I totally set you up that time (see 'Pitch a story')? First I told you to write a blog, and then I told you not to because it's bullshit. And you wondered whether I'm just a crazy man who sets his own chest hair on fire, or whether I actually have some super secret insider juju to lay on you.

Let's go back to that. I wonder which one it'll be?

(Spoiler: a little from Column A, and a little from Column B.)

Yes, you still have to tend your blog. For all the reasons I told you, but also for the practical reason that the barriers to entry, the set-up costs of a blog, are virtually zero. (Except for your time, of course. But when you're starting out the only person who assigns any value to that is you.)

Still, it is a helluva lot of time and even expense, if you

end up travelling, or eating out, or buying a metric shit-tonne of knock-off Manolo Blahniks for your shoe-fetish blog. Sure would be nice to get paid for that, wouldn't it? After all, that's why you're stalking book publishers and crawling in through the bedroom windows of magazine editors to leave notes on their pillows, written in a light pink tincture of your blood and tears, begging for a chance. Just one lousy goddamned chance. You'd like to get paid for this one day.

Well you can. Not a lot, not at first. But you can turn those blog posts into a cash machine with a little bit of extra work, and not by running sketchy weight-loss banner ads on your site.

One of the real suckage points of blogging is getting readers to your site. There are hundreds of millions of blogs or websites or whatever you want to call them stinking up the internet right now. Why should anybody turn up at your dodgy, two-bit operation?

Instead of burying your brilliant prose in some festering sinkhole on the edge of the internet's outer wastelands, think about putting it somewhere people go to get their reading on every day.

Amazon. Or iBooks. Or even Kobo.

When a punter logs into Amazon, chances are they've already made the decision to buy. They went there – or to one of the other online stores – intending to get a book. (Or, yes, a giant vibrating butt plug, but let's assume they're using Amazon for its original purpose: shopping for books about giant vibrating butt plugs). No, they probably didn't go looking for you or your writing, but that doesn't mean you can't lure them into a purchase. The difference between the big online stores and your sad little website is that millions of potential customers visit the stores every day. You don't have to attract them to your site. You just have to go where they are.

I'll talk specifically about Amazon because the Beast of Bezos is probably the purest expression of online book pimping, but the general principles hold true across all the net-based retailers. The thing you have to keep at the front of your mind about Amazon – and I mean this, nail it there, with big rusty nails that punch all the way through your forehead and plunge deep into the cerebellum – the thing you have to remember is that Amazon is not a bookshop. It's a search engine for people who want to spend money.

When you approach it as a search engine, when you forget about it as the digital equivalent of your friendly neighbourhood bookstore, and instead think of it as a vast and hungry silicon carnivore, teetering on the edge of achieving true sentience and enslaving us all, you're a little bit closer to making a few bucks out of it.

Before you can start earning those sweet, sweet Bezos bucks, however, you have to get your shit on the shelf. Or in front of the algorithm. Or whatever.

The process of writing a blog, or throwing a few stories online, is no more complicated than mooching down to the local coffee shop, scrawling a couple of lines of terrible so-called poetry into an old notebook and calling yourself a misunderstood genius. It's piss easy. Self-publishing an ebook? Not so much. At least not if you want to do it properly.

Let's break it down.

There's the writing.

Well, duh.

How about we take that as a given.

But then there's the publishing bit and it's not as simple as firing up your little WordPress blog. It can be very simple if you want to have somebody else do most of the work for you. Author services like Smashwords or Draft2Digital will take your manuscript as a Word document and turn it into an ebook file. They'll even submit it to all, or most, of the online stores. But they'll take a cut of your royalties, assuming you're charging anything, and not every self-publishing service can offer access to every online bookstore. At the time of writing, for instance, Draft2Digital did not have a deal with Amazon to submit books for the Kindle store.

Before you get anywhere near publication though, you should make sure you're not trying to publish total shit. Sure, some people make elephant bucks doing just that. But you're not Stephenie Meyer. You're gonna do this properly and the world is gonna be spared another terrible sparkly vampire infestation.

PSEUDONYMS

There are legit reasons you might use a name other than your own. Your name might suck. Your name might be on the watch list at CIA headquarters because of that time you ran that terrorist cell, or at the checkout of your local Aldi because you've been passing bad cheques. Maybe you are a prize-winning economist who would like to write tentacle porn. Maybe you are a hugely successful pornographer with some fascinating theories about the relative return on investment versus the growth of real wages in a shrinking economy.

In these cases, sure, use a made-up name. Otherwise, what are you embarrassed about? If your book is good enough to put out there in the world, it should go out with your name on it.

There are three pain points you have to get through before you can sell your first ebook. Editing, artwork and formatting.

First, editing. Nothing worth reading ever escaped the gimlet eye of a cruel and censorious editor. I like to think of editing as defence-in-depth against hordes of angry super-entitled readers swarming over your battlements in a killing rage because you misspelled a word or got something wrong. Editors protect us from our natural enemy, the reader. (Joke! It's a joke, people. Sheesh. So uptight). But they also protect us from ourselves. And we truly are our own nemeses.

Editors don't just correct your spelling. (Technically, proofreaders do that. And internet pedants.) Editors work at both the macro and micro level. When you submit a manuscript, the first report you get from your editor is structural. If storylines aren't going anywhere, if characters are flat, if the whole thing sucks like the hard vacuum of space, they'll tell you that you've done very well and pat you on the head and say, 'But if you'd like this book to be just a little bit more awesome, perhaps you could look at …'

When I submitted the first draft for *Leviathan* I'd been reworking the opening section for years. It ran to 60 000 words and it was perfect. There had probably never been a better first chapter written in the history of the English language and certainly not in any of those other loser languages. I couldn't imagine how you could delete or even move a single word. When my editor, Julia Stiles, was done with me, we'd binned 20 000 words from that section alone. There were three others behind it.

When I wrote *Weapons of Choice* I came to the job with half a dozen books to my name. The hell did I have to learn about writing books by this point? So, after thoroughly fucking up the first draft ('Come here, John, and have a pat on the head, you've done so very well, but if you'd like this book to be just a little bit more awesome …') I worked with my editors Steve Saffel and Brianne Tunnicliffe for another 18 months to deliver a manuscript that would not poison my family name unto the seventh generation with its toxic arse juice.

I've lost track of the number of magazine articles published under my name that should have been credited to the long-suffering editors who made them worth reading. Even quick, one-off columns can be improved by the stern blue pencil of correction – or by Track Changes since nobody files hard copy any more. But the stern blue pencil of correction still sounds cooler.

The point of this mea culpa is to convince you that even though you are undoubtedly a genius and one day we will all worship graven images of your likeness and read from your profound masterworks in the town square, you could use some editing. If you want to trouser a wedge of the folding stuff from sales of your self-published ebooks, you need an editor.

You might have got away with typos and poor writing on your blog, but nobody paid to read your stuff there. They'll put up with lower standards because of that. If you want to repackage a year's worth of blog posts as an ebook, however, even punters who paid a lousy 99 cents are going to brain spasm over an unedited manuscript. The same goes for original work. Nobody cares how much blood you leaked through your fingertips writing this thing. If you have more than four or five typos in an average ebook – let's call it 30 000 words, novella length – if you leave plot holes unfilled, characters undeveloped and narrative threads dangling, you're gonna amass an embarrassing number of one-star reviews.

Get an editor.

Okay. I understand. You can't afford an editor. Those bastards are hella expensive. They like to buy the soft toilet paper and they only ever dine on the best generic hamburger-in-a-can, which is why they need the soft toilet paper.

But don't panic. Breathe deeply. We can cut your editorial costs way the hell back. The first step is to find a writing buddy, some other poor deluded fool bitten by the same scribble bug as you. A writing buddy is like a gym buddy, but not as smelly. A writing buddy is someone who keeps you honest, keeps you going back to the keyboard and, most importantly, tells you when you're writing shit. When you choose your writing buddy, make it somebody whose opinion about writing you respect. Doesn't have to be a professor of old Icelandic literature. Someone like you, someone starting out, who knows their way around a sentence, will do. You don't have to talk to your writing buddy every day, but you should check in once a week, just to touch base, and you should get together online or in person once more each week to swap whatever work you've done and have at it with the stern blue pencil of correction.

Some people trust their partner or spouse to read these raw, early drafts but I'd recommend against it. It can be painful, taking criticism of your writing. Probably best you don't sleep next to the first person to perform a tear-down on your little masterpiece. The temptation to smother them at three in the morning can come upon you with surprising intensity.

With your writing buddy, though, you can be honest. 'The first draft of anything is shit', Ernest Hemingway tells us. Go into the deal knowing that, accepting it, and finding a place with your buddy where you can be as hard on each other's words as you are gentle with each other's feelings. You want to be writers. You're going to have to get used to people telling you what you've written is shit. Even worse, you're going to have to get used to them being right, and doing something about it.

If you don't have a single person you'd feel comfortable inviting to be your writing buddy, you could try a writing group. There are some great writing groups around, and some amazing books have come out of them. If finding a single writing buddy is likely to be a challenge, though, how much more difficult will be finding half a dozen writing buds who won't want to murder each other with pillows at three in the morning? Two writers critiquing each other's work implies a level of trust not often found in normal life. Six or seven writers? Sounds like a case for Miss Marple.

Still, if you want to go down that path, your local Writers Centre will have contacts for groups you can ask to join. Alternately they'll have resources for you to set up your own.

When you have your first draft to the point where you could show it to someone other than your writing buddy without unreasonable fear of suffering a prolapsed anus from the humiliation, it's time for beta readers. These don't have to be other writers – in fact, it's better if they're not. If you've been running a blog for a while, or have any kind of normal profile online, however limited, you should be able to put together a small group of people who are happy to read whatever you've written and offer some feedback. Generalist readers are great, pedants are awesome, but if anyone brings special skills to the mix they could be your new best friend.

I recently sent an ebook out to my betas and was stoked to discover that one of them had a forensic medical background. His tweaking of the autopsy on the eight-foot-tall demon improved it so much I made him a character in an upcoming space opera. This is one of the nice things about having good betas; over time you can build up trust and rewarding relationships that have nothing to do with a payday. Some people just like to read things early, and everyone loves a cameo.

Now for the part you're not gonna love.

Even though your writing bud and your betas have cleaned up that manuscript, scrubbed it until its cheeky little belly button shines, it still needs a pro edit if you intend to ask people to pay for it. Hell, I'd send my manuscript off for a professional clean-up even if I was giving it away as a brand-building exercise. You can't build your name on typos and fuck-ups.

So, how do you find an editor and how much will you pay?

A professional industry standard edit will cost you at least 50 or 60 bucks an hour.

Wait!

Don't run!

There's a but …

If you have taken the time to prepare your manuscript for editing, if you're not sending her a steaming pile of old poop wrap, your editor will have a lot less work to do. And she is a professional. She's not going to fuck you around. Her rep is her business and her business is always in need of new projects to edit.

If you're worried about costs blowing out, get an estimate, put a cap on what you can afford to spend. You might be making art, but you're also running a business. Act like it. But you will still need to spend something. You are not good enough to send a book straight from your hard drive onto the open market. I am not good enough. Nobody is.

Where to find your editor, then?

Luckily, it's not too hard. Resources like *The Australian Writer's Marketplace* are full of them, sharpened pencils poised to plunge into your fluttering heart. Internationally the difficulties of the publishing industry have meant hundreds, maybe thousands of editors losing jobs in-house and putting their shingle out for work on the internet. Many of them have found the freelance life to be a lot more rewarding, and because the net has basically collapsed the concept of distance into meaninglessness, at least for the exchange of information, there is no reason your editor cannot be sitting in Montreal or Edinburgh, while you crank out the awesome in Rooty Hill.

All of these resources are a Google search away, but if you want to be all methodical like, you could start with the websites of the various recognised international bodies: the Society of Editors and Proofreaders; the Association of Freelance Editors, Proofreaders and Indexers; and the Editorial Freelancers Association.

As the big publishers sacked more and more of their talent – yeah sacked them, *shit-canned* them, let's call it what it is, rather than some anodyne bullshit like 'outsourcing' – that talent began to gather elsewhere. Their heartless downsizing is your opportunity. There are now plenty of online businesses connecting writers to editorial professionals. Some are pure minty-fresh new economy, like Reedsy and Bibliocrunch. Others, like the Independent Editors Group, reek of tweed and leather armchairs, and if you have to ask for their price list you can't afford them.

And some look like mad, bad, dangerous fun. Yeah, I'm looking at you, the Book Butchers: 'We slaughter your writing, so it can rise in glory from the ashes'.

Do you want to spend $3000–$4000 having your blog posts edited into publishable shape? Not really. So maybe pay attention when you're writing them in the first place, go to your trusted betas for the de facto edit, and ask your old high school English teacher or favourite maiden aunt to check your spelling.

But if you want to try your hand at self-publishing fiction, or long-form nonfiction, grit your teeth and get ready to spend some money. Budget for 10 cents a word on an edit that covers structural, line and copy editing.

Now, onto artwork.

No, you can't do your own artwork either.

Why? Because kindlecoverdisasters.tumblr.com is why.

Go on, I don't mind. Go and have a look. I'll be here when you get back.

...

...

...

... Oh hai! You're back then? Yeah, the one about the paranormal sex clown, that was my fave too, and far from the worst in class.

Readers will slam your book closed if it is poorly written, but they won't even open it if you can't get the cover right. And you can't. Trust me.

You do have options though, and they run from the disgracefully cheap (but still quite nice) to the ruinously expensive (but still very nice).

The cheap option: Failed Covers R Us dot com. Okay, that's not an actual business but it should be. In fact, excuse me for a second while I grab up the domain name.

Alrighty. I'm back (with an exciting new business idea).

You can get the artwork for a book cover for less than 50 bucks, depending on how the Aussie dollar, aka the Pacific Peso, is trending on the exchange rates. Sites such as Go On Write and Humble Nations offer solid generic artwork that won't embarrass you at Ye Olde

Kindle Shoppe. There are hundreds of indie graphic designers offering these services and most will also sell you a bespoke cover if you cross their palm with silver. Indeed, one of the dark secrets of the trade publishing industry is the number of titles from big-name houses coming out wrapped in cheap-arse covers bought from bulk-art warehouses. It's like the restaurant which charges you four or five bucks for your coffee, fresh from the fucking Nespresso.

'Yes, of course our barista put the pod in all by himself.'

Another alternative I've found useful is to host a design contest at a site such as 99Designs. You offer a price for a winning design and graphic artists submit their proposed artwork. Not everyone loves this process, because only the winning artist gets paid. They have a point, but writers also have to produce sample chapters and long, detailed outlines for submissions to publishers who might not decide to commission their work. God knows my bottom drawer holds more than a few orphaned proposals for novels and series that never got past acquisition. Nobody forced me to write them. I look at writing those failed pitches like any business would look at tendering for work on the open market: a cost you have to factor in.

I'll explain the process at 99D, but you can generalise and apply it to any commission you might offer a cover artist.

The more information you provide in your design brief, the closer to your imagined ideal the proposals will be. The same holds when you're commissioning artwork directly from a designer. My first attempt at running a cover-art contest was hopeless, but the friendly folk at 99Designs gave me a few tips which helped a lot.

Just as the designers are competing for you, you are competing for their attention. A good contest title draws the eye and sparks the interest. My first effort was simply the name of the story I wanted illustrated: 'Here Be Monsters'. Great title for a story, but not for a design contest. It told them nothing. But 'Old versus new illustrative ebook cover for famed Australian author – Zombies, time travel and the First Fleet!' provided information about the job with the ego-stroking implication that maybe some of that 'fame' might rub off *(hahahahahaha)*.

A subtitle – 'Time travelling zombie stomping First Fleet action' – delivers more information about the content and also ticks a few boxes for the book's metadata entries later on (more about this in the next section).

In 'content details', I provided a description of the ebook in the form of a blurb: 'In *Here Be Monsters* the First Fleet which colonised Australia in 1788 is about to make landfall when a mysterious storm deposits the future city of Sydney on top of them. It is full of zombies which attack the Fleet.'

And finally in 'other', a catch-all section for general notes about the project, I gave the designers as much information as I could about the aesthetics and specifications.

The cover should lean more towards fun than horror.

THOUGHTS ON THE COVER:

I want to show a battle between Jane Austen type ladies and gentlemen vs modern day zombies on the deck of an old wooden ship to the backdrop of Sydney (the Sydney Opera House & Harbour Bridge).

FOR EXAMPLE:

• women using parasols (vintage umbrellas) as weapons

• 18th-century marines fighting with a musket

• half-naked modern woman firing 20th century machine guns.

WHAT WE WANT:

We want the juxtaposition between old and new in a fluid and dynamic way.

This juxtaposition of old and new is the sort of thing Eric Flint and SM Stirling do on their book covers. See ATTACHED cover art.

TEXT REQUIRED ON THE COVER:

Title: Here Be Monsters

Author: John Birmingham

SPECS:

Finished art as JPEG.

Front cover only

2500 pixels tall by 1563 pixels wide

Max file size 2MB

I swear to God the half-naked chick firing the assault rifle is totally integral to the story. The more you specify the imagery you're after, the more specific images a graphic artist will provide.

The specs are important because this file needs to sit on the servers at Amazon, iBooks, Kobo and maybe half a dozen other smaller retailers. Ebooks don't have back covers, so tell your artist you don't need one. The pixel dimensions are standard and won't cause your artwork to be chopped off halfway through the title. The file size is crucial because you can be charged data fees for anything over two megs. If you sell a million copies – and I'm sure you will – you really don't want to have to pay for all those downloads.

Now you have your artwork and your clean manuscript, what next?

Formatting.

Are you a code monkey? Do you fart out a rich cloud of html when you wake up in the morning? If not then maybe don't try formatting your ebook for yourself.

If you absolutely must try coding your own ebook, have a read of Guido Henkel's *Zen of eBook Formatting*, which is a commendably simple introduction to the subject.

Then just hire Guido to do the job for you, like I did. Alternatively you could sign over a small percentage of any royalty you make to a service like Smashwords and let them worry about it. Even then, however, you still have to submit a Word document that complies with their style guide.

Long story short: The deeper you get into the forest the easier it is to get lost. If you're coming at your first indie publishing project as a complete noob, I'd advise you to use one of the self-publishing service bureaus that take a cut of your royalty. You pay nothing upfront so you've lost nothing but time if the whole thing tanks.

But let's try to avoid that happening.

FIND YOUR READERS AND MAKE THEM PAY

There's been a lot of bullshit written and talked about self-publishing by a lot of people with vested interests. I'll try not to add to the steaming pile.

Bottom line, yes, you can make money publishing your own stuff. Small print after the tiny asterisk on the bottom line: I have no fucking idea how much money. Partly that's down to you. How well you throw words on the page. How savvy you are about selling them.

We're going to assume you have a base level of competence. You might have completed a three- or four-year degree in creative writing, or spent the last few years grubbing around online or freelancing in hard copy. But you want to make a bit more of the folding stuff from it.

You have 30000–40000 words you think you can sell. Hell, you might even have a couple of full-length novels. But you're competing with millions of other books. You're not JK Rowling or Stephen King. You don't have your own army of fans and no publisher is going to be taking out big honking adverts for you on the side of buses or on billboards along the freeway to the airport.

That's okay, you're not alone. Even most published authors struggle to get attention for their books. The main publishing houses all maintain large publicity and marketing departments, but their resources are finite. Not everyone is going to get the platinum package. You sell a lot of books for them and they'll spend a lot of money selling even more books for you. It's a virtuous circle, unless you're hunkered down outside of it, shivering in the cold, spending your days answering email questionnaires and writing thousand-word guest posts for obscure blogs and book review sites because your 12-year-old publicist thought it might help, and because Stephen King sucked up your publisher's entire travel budget.

(I'm joking about the King. I think he flies everywhere in his own jumbo jet.)

You can and should invest some time in building your social media following, because it's a channel you control, but it's a social channel, not a commercial one. Twitter, Facebook, Instagram, whatever succeeds them, their impact on sales figures is pretty ephemeral, but they do allow you to stay in contact with readers. That contact may be light, fleeting and an uncertain foundation on which to build a business, but it has its uses which we'll talk about later (see 'Use the media').

What you really need, though, is something like those adverts on the side of the metro buses telling people that your book is out, go buy it. You need a form of advertising with a little more punch than those desperate fucking Tweet storms screaming, 'Buy MY #AWESOME Tingly #Werewolf #ROMANCE ebook', that blow through my timeline every couple of hours. Most people aren't interested and if you persist they will unfollow or even block you across multiple platforms. Twitter, Facebook, even your precious blog? All bullshit. Well, not totally, but they're not much use when it comes to separating the punters from their funds.

How then to amass a collection of readers who actually want to know when your next tingly werewolf romance is out so they can give you their money? Oddly enough, they will come to you if you lay the right bait. Oops. Did I say bait? Oh dear me, I meant incentive. Yes, with the right incentive they will wander like naive fools into the fearsome trap you laid for them with the snapping jaws and the rusted teeth.

[Insert maniacal laugh here.]

So, the incentive, the bait, what is it?

Free stuff. The magical fairy dust which is the currency of the internet. You're going to borrow your business model from the likes of Google, who give something away (search engine, email, other people's copyrighted material) in return for something valuable (your personal details and immortal soul).

All those short stories you've published on your blog, that novel you released chapter by chapter on Wattpad, the thoughtful essays you gave for free to the internet billionaires who own Medium, take them down, take them down now! You need enough material to fill a book. Luckily, it's just an ebook so a decent 10 000 words will do it, but if you have more, great.

You go through the process I explained a few minutes ago to get your ebook into the various online retailers, but you don't charge for this one. You give it away and you give it away hard; really pimp that thing on whatever meagre channels you already control. Right up the front of the book, and at the back, immediately after the last page, you invite people to get another free book if they liked this one.

Yeah, you're gonna need another book, sorry about that. But again, you can get away with a well-produced novella or piece of short-form nonfiction. Be aware, though, the more perceived value that you offer, the more substantial the freebie, the tastier the bait will be.

Your readers can have this second title for free as long as you get their email – for your mailing list. The mailing list that you will lovingly tend to and build up into a retail channel that you alone control. On this list you will amass hundreds, eventually thousands, even tens of thousands of readers who have volunteered to hear from you when you have something to tell them or sell them.

Wanna see mine? www.jbismymasternow.com

Let's recap.

- Give away a book for free because people are cheap-arse punks who cannot resist the lure of the freebie.

- Place prominent links to your mailing list sign-up page in the front and back of said freebie.

- Harvest their souls.

If that seems confusingly simple, it's because it is. The machinery of landing pages and funnels and magnets and ... well ... all of it, the machinery can take a while to set up and often involves paying highly skilled code monkeys to design multiple layers of the Matrix for you. Until yesterday.

I'm not being metaphorical.

As I was writing this chapter, girding my enormous loins to launch into a long and tedious technical discussion of the architecture and engineering needed to give away books and collect email addresses, some other writer solved that problem. Actually, it was a bunch of other writers, most of them self-published indie authors, calling themselves BookFunnel.

What are they? A delivery service for writers. If you have a free book, a time-travelling, zombie-stomping alternate history, let's say, and you want to offer it to yo' peeps in return for their subscription to an email list,

BookFunnel simplifies the whole process. Massively.

Before BookFunnel, when it came time to give away *Here Be Monsters*, my time-travelling, zombie-stomping alternate history, I was looking at having to host multiple copies of the file in multiple formats on a server costing me a couple of hundred bucks a year. Yeah, I could have used Dropbox or Google Docs, but I wanted my own server.

A reader would sign up for my mailing list, and by the magic of the interwebz hundreds of tiny little leprechauns I hold captive in the bowels of my iMac would send them a link for their freebie. The reader would download it and then side-load it to whatever device they preferred for their reading. Inevitably, invariably, with enough people downloading it, dozens, maybe hundreds, would have issues with the file transfer. And they'd be emailing me about it.

Not any more.

I've road-tested BookFunnel. I've been using it for months now. It's gold. It works exactly as advertised. I give you the link, you hit it up, you get the book in the right format on your device or desktop. If you have a problem, that's BookFunnel's to deal with, not mine, and they have a call centre of actual live leprechauns to sort you out. Would it be inappropriate if I told you that just talking about this technology gives me an author stiffy you could crack fleas on?

Okay then, we'll never speak of that again.

If you're like me and you prefer a couple of levels of

redundancy and back-up, you can still get old school with your mailing list sign-up tech, just in case BookFunnel doesn't work out. (I know, right? An internet-based business that doesn't work out? Don't make me roll my eyes.)

In that case, or if you're just interested in the archeology of indie publishing, I recommend you read any or all of the following three books. They predate BookFunnel, and until it went live they were among the best resources a self-published writer could call on:

- *Let's Get Digital: How to Self-Publish and Why You Should* by David Gaughran

- *Reader Magnets: Get Readers to Come to You* by Nick Stephenson

- *Write. Publish. Repeat: The No-Luck-Required Guide to Self-Publishing Success* by Sean Platt and Johnny B Truant with David Wright.

Gaughran is probably the most hard-headed of them, and he is pretty good at updating and revising his text to account for changes in the industry and technology. Stephenson is less an author than a force of nature who will blow in through your front door if you open it even a little bit, then he'll tear around your house like a money-making tornado who can't understand why you don't make as much money as him.

Platt, Truant and Wright are foul-mouthed and funny, and if you're too cheap to pay for their book you could do worse than listening to their excellent work on *The Self-Publishing Podcast*. It's sweary but informative.

Seriously, though, just buy the books, you cheap bastard. They get right down into the weeds of this business in a way I can't hope to in just one chapter.

Right, let's get into the weeds: categories, metadata and search-engine optimisation (SEO). Did you notice how all those book I just mentioned had long, clunky subtitles? Even my giveaway ebook, the soul catcher for my email list, isn't just *Here Be Monsters*. It's *Here Be Monsters: a time-travelling, zombie-stomping alternate history*.

Why?

Because reasons!

Specifically you have to remember that Amazon is not a bookshop. It's a search engine. When you put your product on the virtual shelves, you get to nominate *where* it should be shelved. The tens of millions of readers searching Amazon and its competitors don't always know exactly what they want. If they like crime novels they might just search for crime. If they like a sub-genre of crime, say, heists or kidnaps, they might search in those categories. When you put your wares up for sale, you get to nominate a few examples of where your book might best be 'shelved'. You need a category where there is some activity, where people are buying, but not one where the entire first page of results is owned by

Stephenie Meyer or JK Rowling.

Nick Stephenson is very good at explaining how to work that system, and if you get his book you'll very quickly be sucked into the dizzying vortex of his video training series. Remember when I called him a force of nature blowing in through your front door and tear-arsing around like a money-making tornado?

I was doing the opposite of exaggerating.

One way of tweaking the search engine to get a little more selling power is to use a subtitle to get your book into a few more categories. So people looking for time-travel novels or zombie stories or alternate history are more likely to be served up *Here Be Monsters* simply because of the subtitle. The three indie publishing guides I recommended above all have subtitles that read like Google searches for this reason.

You can work the same algorithmic machinery to pump your reviews and sales. Let's say you've built your mailing list to just under 2000 subscribers – the point at which a service like MailChimp stops being free and starts being a tax-deductible business expense. It's time to launch your book. Do you just throw it out there and bang on a big tin yelling, 'Come and git it, yer lousy good fer nuthin' …'

Obviously not. That was a leading question.

Entice and reward early subscribers to your list by keeping them on a high-sugar diet of freebies. That's right, you're going to give away more of your precious shit. There are many ways of doing this but a simple one is to quietly release the book into the wild, free for 24 hours. Let the first 100 or 200 subscribers to your list know that it's there, and that since you already own their immortal souls you won't be requiring payment if they get in quick. A very gentle nudge in the direction of having them leave a review will probably see you pick up a swag of four- and five-star reviews from grateful readers which will be sitting there to impress the buying public when you increase the price to full retail and blast out the announcement to half your mailing list. Three or four days later you hit the other half. By splitting the list like this you spread your sales over a couple of days, avoiding the artificial spike in popularity that most online bookstores have learned to filter out via their software.

The following week you could hit up your social media channels. The week after that, if you have any money to spend on Facebook or BookBub advertising, that's when to splurge. The online stores all reward consistent sales growth over time. After a certain point they will begin to do your work for you, pushing your title out to a much vaster audience than you could hope to reach on your own.

These tips alone should be enough to start moving book sales for you, but if you want to do a deep dive into the topic, and you should, I would again recommend David Gaughran as your guide, this time contemplating the rare and lyrical beauty of *Let's Get Visible: How to Get Noticed and Sell More Books*.

PIMP YOUR BOOK

Used to be that you wrote the book and somebody else took care of the vile commercial unpleasantness of selling it. Those happy days are over. In the exciting go-go world of modern publishing we are all pimps now. You see some sad fucking shit when you've signed up with a publisher and talk turns to marketing and publicity. Get ready to humiliate yourself.

ENDORSEMENTS

Oh man. I don't wanna do this. But, deep breath, here goes. Yes, it does help if you can get some sort of endorsement from another, bigger writer, on your cover. If you have a publisher, they'll often send out an early version of your manuscript to other writers who might be interested in providing a quote. More likely, however, they'll leave the whole noxious business to you.

Let's say you would like an endorsement from me. How you gonna get that? I doubt you have the promotional budget for all the hookers and blow it would normally take to convince me to give you a reach around. So unless you know me personally – by which I mean we are actual friends, not Facebook Friends – you got some hard work ahead of you, Jack.

You somehow have to convince me to take time, which I don't have, out of my daily schedule, which is a crushing hell of conflicting commitments, to read a big enough chunk of your manuscript that I won't embarrass myself by endorsing it.

This is why most writers just say no. Endorsements are work, actual goddamned work, for which we don't get paid, and which stops us from doing our real work. There, I said it. Our real work.

A few tips, then.

Your chances of getting the endorsement you want are minimal. Accept that.

Don't stalk the writer.

Don't mug the writer, jumping out from behind a tree and whacking them upside the head with your bloody manuscript.

Never, ever go to their house. A poet did this to me

once. I thought it was a home invasion, but it was worse. It was a poet.

Do your work. If you expect somebody to do you the favour of putting their name on your book, you can do them the favour of getting to know them. It's not that hard these days. Do they have a blog, Facebook page, a Twitter handle, some other point of contact with their fans and readers? Then you should be there a long, long time before you turn up on the front doorstep with your thick bundle of handwritten poetry and your uncomfortably insistent, creepy demands for a cover line.

This is much easier to do if you are working with a trade publisher. They'll get you invited to festivals. They will take you to dinner and drinks with the other grown-up writers, and as long as you are not a complete head case, you will be welcomed into the big, loving dysfunctional family that is publishing. You will get to know who is cool, and who is an insufferable cock-chafer. You will get to make that personal approach. Even then, you need to accept that you're asking for a big fucking favour and it just may not be possible for your chosen writer to deliver. Be gracious. Move on. It's not about you.

If you are coming at this from the world of indie publishing, it's different but the same. Indie publishing is its own world, with its own culture, its own ways, its meeting places and songlines. Join the discussion boards, pop into the chat rooms on the podcasts, engage the people whose work you like, get to know them, and then strike like a spitting cobra of death.

Long story short, don't expect strangers to do you a favour.

'Get author book jacket photos taken now, while you're young. And get the negatives and copyright on those photos.'
– Chuck Palahniuk

BOOK SIGNINGS

They can feel something like falling backwards into an open-cut mine full of cocaine-dusted Easter bunnies, or something which is not quite so much fun. The best book signing I ever had was an accident. I wandered into a Dymocks bookshop in a Westfield to, you know, buy a book. Somebody recognised me and asked if I would sign a copy of *Felafel* for them. Somebody else came up and wanted their copy signed. Three hours later the mall was closing around us and I was still signing copies, now being brought in from other stores just to meet demand. Why did that happen? No fucking idea. Maybe because Father's Day was the next day and people saw a chance for an unusual gift.

And on the flipside? I once did a signing at Berkelouw Books in Darlinghurst with Linda Jaivin. It was around about the same time, actually. We each had two books in the top ten. *Tasmanian Babes* and *Felafel* for me. *Eat*

Me and *Rock and Roll Babes from Outer Space* for Linda. We were selling thousands and thousands of books each week. The bookshop guys thought it would be a good idea to have us do a joint session. It was a great idea. Three people turned up.

A professional doesn't sweat that shit. A professional signs all the copies in the store anyway, because the bookshop can't return them after you've scrawled inside the cover.

It's a hideous, fearful time the hour or so before a book signing. You really have zero fucking idea whether anybody will even show up. My advice: avoid them if you can. Sure, visit the store, schmooze the staff, sign a couple of copies in the back room. But nothing reeks of desperate failure so much as an author with flop sweat sitting at his little card table, grinning his shit-eating grin, waiting for someone to stray close enough to trip up and hold down with an arm lock or a choke until they agree to buy a book. We've all been there. Well, okay, probably not JK Rowling. But the rest of us have, and you will too. If you get guilt-tripped into doing one of these things, take a friend. Take two or three, so they can tag team each other, engaging you in empty, slightly despairing small talk so you don't look as big a loser as you feel.

Or, you know, just do the back-room visit like I suggested.

HOW TO BE INTERVIEWED

Assume the interviewer has not read your book. They haven't. If you're on television or radio try to answer their ignorant fucking questions without making them seem like a mouth-breathing Cletus who married his cousin and played banjo with his toes at the reception. Be gracious. Be generous. Flatter this egomaniac as though it is they not you who has the Nobel Prize for Literature (or would have, were it not for that fucking Vargas Llosa). And make sure to mention the name of your book at least eight times.

If you are dealing with a print journalist, expect the same three or four questions you got from every other print journalist. Don't be afraid to simply repeat your wittiest answers, which you will get to practise again and again. And remember you are not talking to them, you are talking to their audience. They are simply the filter you have to get through.

REVIEWS

A really scorching review in a respected broadsheet newspaper can sink a literary novel or a high-tone piece of nonfiction. A really great review might move a few hundred copies, but not much more. Half a dozen great reviews? Yeah, that'd help, but how does knowing that help you? You can't make those reviews happen, even by writing a great book. Reviewing is subjective and fraught at best, and corrupt and vindictive more often than you'd care to know. The buzz we're looking for doesn't come from reviews. It's more of a cloud of discussion now. A mention in some insufferable *Guardian* op-ed. A reference by Tommy Gleeson on *The Weekly*. Condemnation under parliamentary privilege by some tosser in the outer ministry at the very least.

As for your reviews, don't sweat them in the particular, worry about them in general. It really is a matter of 'Never mind the quality, feel the length'. Where reviews count is online and en masse. Reader reviews at Amazon, iBooks and the other digital stores provide a crowdsourced guarantee that individual write-ups in the mainstream media cannot. One of the reasons for building a mailing list, besides having a marketing and communication channel you alone control, is to have a group of readers you can rely on to provide reviews.

Grow that list. Farm it like a boss.

USE SOCIAL MEDIA

As with so many things in life – okay, toilets, I'm talking about toilets – I fell into Twitter by accident. Having lunch with a friend who was a bona-fucking-fide social media guru long before we all became social media gurus, he told me to get my arse onto Twitter and grab up my name before somebody else did. Good advice, as it turned out. Within a couple of weeks of registering my account as @JohnBirmingham, a fake John Birmingham had also registered.

I was stoked, identity theft being the sincerest form of flattery. But unfortunately fake John Birmingham's tweets petered out, buried by an avalanche of my own. I became entranced with Twitter. And then I became entranced with drunk Twitter. And in the end I became, I like to think, a gold-medal-winning champion at Drunk Airport Twitter.

I got sucked into the Twitterz, partly as an epic time waster and partly because of its potential to amplify the buzz we're all so fucking desperate to create in the two or three weeks after a book first appears on the shelves. Twitter, it seemed to me, way more than Facebook, was word of mouth raised to the power of lots and lots. (Facebook has since taken the crown).

It was also a trap for both the naive and the coldly calculating alike. The conversational nature of all social media is almost perfectly designed to lead people into saying things they shouldn't in public. Intimacy and immediacy get it on in a way that can lead the unwary to forget that they're actually taking their pants off in front of the whole world. My former colleague at Fairfax Media Mike Carlton ran afoul of this when he got into a pissing match with some readers who'd taken offence at a column he'd written about Israel. By this, I mean to say he ran afoul of Fairfax's nemesis, News Corp. They republished and revelled in his two-fisted exchanges, feigning outrage and complaining of a dizzying attack of the vapours because a bitter rival was employing such a cad and bounder as this Carlton fellow. It was egregious hypocrisy, of course, News being the home of the worst trollumnists in the world, but it worked. Through a series of misadventures and miscalculations, Mike found himself a 'former columnist', and all because he'd given as good as he got to a bunch of shitheads who were sitting up, begging for it.

Falling for troll bait is only one potential downside of living your writing life online. At the other end of the scale there are those spivs and pimps who are only too aware of the potential for monetising our online conversations but who are, unfortunately for them, clueless and incapable of restraining their slobbering desire to cash in on this potential. They come in all forms. From the barking hucksters trying to sell you their latest author training course ('I will make you a Google ad ninja!') to the clueless mush-heads tweeting their own endorsements of their own self-published novel a hundred times a week, usually to 57 followers, half of whom are politicians or porn stars who followed back automatically and never check their own fucking timeline anyway.

It is possible, though, to use social media to promo your work without coming off as an amphetamine-crazed greed head or a fallen Nigerian cabinet minister with access to unexplained funds that could be remitted into your bank account this very afternoon, were you to trust him with your wallet and PIN.

It's not for everyone. And if you're going to do social media, you have to be genuine about it. That doesn't mean you can't go online to hawk your wares, but the defining characteristic of social media is that it is social, not commercial. If you want people to take an interest in you, unless you are a mega-celebrity, you will need to take at least a passing interest in them, which means actually following the conversations, occasionally contributing to them, and not drowning them out with a wall of sound composed of nothing but sales announcements.

Just so you know, the publicity department of your average publisher considers a wall of sound composed of nothing but sales announcements a really sexy fucking deal. Increasingly they expect writers to do pretty much all their publicity online. They're not being dim. It's just how business works. The screw only turns one way and the rise of social media has meant shrinking budgets for traditional media campaigns, which is a shame, because a lot of writers are hopeless at online.

I would say I'm stunned by the number of writers who are complete arse at doing social media, but that'd be a damnable lie because most writers are complete arse at being social, period. The skills needed to sit alone in your room, suspended somewhere within an imagined world, are not the same skills needed to go out into the world of real things and sell that world to the book-buying punter.

Genre authors tend to be better at the whole pimpage thing than your big-L literature types, not because we're all BuzzFeedy charlatans but, I think, because at heart most spec fiction writers are hapless fanbois and grrrls who simply cannot help themselves. We are as undone by proximity to our media fetishes as anybody. We get as giddy about a fave new book or TV series as anyone. This is probably why so many of us, like Charlie Stross and John Scalzi, write blogs. Not to sell shit, but to celebrate it.

Blogging was my first foray into really exploring a relationship with my readers independent of my publishers. That sounds kind of skeevy, doesn't it? Like the readers and me were sneaking out in our flared pants and nylon body shirts for some hot 1970s-style orgytastic action while my poor publisher sits at home, listening to *Tapestry* on eight-track while staring through hot tears at a bowl of deep fried camembert and wailing, 'Where is JB? I made his favourite and everything!'

But I didn't start blogging as a marketing exercise, or to get laid. I started blogging because I needed an outlet for storytelling that wasn't related to paying my mortgage or my taxes.

It was a reader called Steve Murphy who got me into it. Murph had written a review of my first thriller, *Weapons of Choice*, on his blog. He liked the book, liked it a lot, but he'd picked up a couple of howlers I made when using military terminology.

Murph proved to be adept at catching other bloopers. Like the time I tried to fire off a rocket launcher in a small room. Apparently you can't do that. You'll hurt yourself, and he let me know. If you are the sort of writer who bristles at being corrected by 'amateurs' like this, I suggest you get the fuck over yourself. (For one thing, Murph isn't an amateur. He did a tour of the Gulf during the first oil war back in the early 1990s. If you're going to have a fact checker, or researcher or even just a beta reader, you want one with mad skills and relevant history like that.) I thanked Murph for reading the book so closely, and offering his critique, and I had my publishers correct my mistakes in the next edition. It was a win for everybody.

Having cashed in on that brief foray into the blogosphere, I figured what the hell, let's kick back here for a while. Setting up my own blog I used it at first as a diary, simply recording my day's work routine, and occasionally discussing the business of writing. I think I attracted a hard-core following of maybe, hell, I don't know, a dozen or so regular readers. This was despite having books that have sold hundreds of thousands of copies. It was the early days of blogging.

But I soon realised that getting online was a way to stay in contact with readers between books and across the vast distances which often separated us. So I kept at it.

With each book the audience grew. It's just not possible to travel everywhere and talk to everyone on a book tour, but as long as we can get together at the Burger (Cheeseburgergothic.com) and talk over the new book, or the old, or someone else's book, or the chances of a *Blake's Seven* remake, or whether *Agents of Shield* is really just the *A-Team* of the new millennium, it hardly matters.

Over time the regulars who established themselves there became more than just readers or blog buddies, they became friends and even collaborators.

Years of tapping away at that blog, of building real friendships with the people who turned up there, prepared me well when I later moved on to Twitter, which became something of an engine room for me. I use it for both my publishing and mass media work like a lot of other writers and journalists. Some of them really understand the nature of Twitter. Some don't.

It is first and foremost a conversation. Not a public address system.

Of course there is a trap in conversation. And it's not just the obvious one of making yourself a target for crazy people. Fuck me, the crazy people. Seriously, what did these people do before the internet? There can't have been that many basements or backwoods cabins to hold them all.

Anyway, as you build up your following it can get distracting, so bad in fact that you never write another book again because you spend all of your time reading and writing fucking tweets.

If I had one piece of advice to offer the serious writer, as opposed to the hapless pretender, it would be to rigorously control the amount of time you spend on social media. It can be an incredibly powerful tool, but it can also be a bottomless time suck. You might want to think about allotting 15 or 20 minutes at the start and end of the day to invest in your online presence and then PULL THE FUCKING PLUG.

For me, the benefits of investing some time building up a reasonable following on Twitter came quickly. For six months while on deadline I posted daily updates of progress, sometimes challenging all comers to a race to see who could reach, say, 2000 words for the day first. It was surprisingly motivating and bracing to kick the arses of would-be writers and English students every day. Worthless punks, the lot of them. [Insert crazy biker laugh here.] Hell, some days taunting would-be writers was all I had to keep me at the keyboard.

As I had at the Burger, I also threw research queries out. This allowed my Twitter peeps to invest in a book long before they could lay hands on the finished copy at full retail. It also meant I spent much less time trawling the net for bullshit arcana such as descriptions of locations I needed for scenes. Example? Unable to find a reliable image or description of the third floor of New York's Plaza Hotel before it was renovated, I turned my first-world problem over to Twitter. Within an hour I had photographs of the hotel from the time period I requested. One reader even scanned a news story about the reno, including before and after shots, and posted it online for me.

When the *Disappearance Trilogy* made it out into the world, and I kicked off touring it, I announced dates and venues a couple of weeks out and invited my Tweetenvolk along. First time I did this I was kinda curious to see what effect it had on numbers, if any. Bottom line, the turnouts at my gigs were much larger, the number of sales greater, and the events themselves much more fun than previous tours. Over the course of a week touring *After America*, I estimated that a couple of hundred extra people attended the gigs and bought books.

Now, sure, in terms of mass market numbers, a couple of hundred extra punters, while good for the individual bookstore running the gig, won't make a big difference to me or my publishers at the end of the financial year. But the amplifying effect of social media isn't restricted to simply getting people out of their living rooms. A lot of those who come to your events will push word of the book out through their own online networks, either as tweets, blogs, Facebook posts or whatever. This is word-of-mouth broadcast at a much greater volume than was previously possible. It won't replace traditional media and marketing strategies, but it does have the potential to improve them.

Finally, in case this should all sound horribly fucking cynical and calculating, I gotta tell you that it's also a helluva lot of fun, especially when the virtual meets up in the real. Instead of a room full of strangers, awkwardly circling each other, most people who turned up on my last book tour knew at least some of the other punters, even if they had never met in the real world. It made for more drinks and rowdier crowd, which, again, can only add to the buzz. On the downside, it did mean more hangovers and an increased Berocca bill.

It was a price I was willing to pay.

And the hangovers were nothing compared to an average day at a writers festival.

ENJOY THE PERKS

I've never understood writers who complain about the festival circuit. Fuck me, what's not to love? You get flown in like James Bond, put up in some plush hotel, fed like a fucking potentate, and over the course of a week you might have to do about 14 minutes 'work', which mostly involves gobbing on about the fascinating fellow who is you to a room full of adoring groupies. Other than that, it's all hookers and blow.

Plenty of blow, if you're the visiting international super author who swept through Sydney a couple of years ago like a tornado through a trailer park. Plenty of blowjobs if you're the handsome, visiting, young literary lion who cut a swathe through the ranks of doe-eyed publishing grrrls at festival after festival, leaving it to his grizzled old agent to explain that the knee trembler out the back of the wharf restaurant was just 'festival sex' and, really, the duly ravished editor, publicist or marketing maven shouldn't plan on a Mills and Boon ending.

In fact, the standard of behaviour amongst overseas authors is so uniformly and despicably lower than the local scribblers, that you could only put it down to being a long way from home and surrounded by strangers, none of whom you plan on ever seeing again.

WRITING PRIZES

Enter them, win them. It's easier than you'd imagine. Not with the big-name, high profile novel-writing prizes. Fuck them. You got Buckley's, kid. But there are hundreds of other smaller prizes on offer, and competition there can be surprisingly thin, even when the lolly that's up for grabs is stupidly generous.

If you ever see any newspapers or magazines running writing competitions, get your shit together and your submission in ASAP. You know the beauty of publisher-sponsored competitions? They have to read what you send them. You're not going into a slush pile. These stupid bastards have actually said to the world of crazy, unpublished writers, 'Come at me, bro'.

If you are any good, you will get through to the final round. I have won these competitions. I have judged these competitions. I speak the truth now; if you have a base level of competence and even the merest flair, you have a better than even chance

of getting into that final round. Once you're there, it's more of a crapshoot. But if you lose one, there's always another one coming right up. Honestly, get on it. Now.

It's not all about the sex, though. There's also the drunkenness. I chose my original agent, Annette Hughes, many years ago because she'd passed out and fallen under the tables at the casino, a vantage point from which I was certain she would understand things from my perspective.

Anyone who spends any time at a festival will eventually see, or trip over, some God of Letters, crawling around on the floor, covered in their own vomit, and possibly taking up-skirt photos with their mobile phone. Do the work, crank out the Pomodoro and it could be you stumbling across the legless Brit Lit genius, being unexpectedly and unwantedly pashed by another, before getting 'belly-butted' outside the dunny by a Nobel Prize–winning Irish poet and novelist, all in short order.

While it's all good fun for we 'umble scribblers, the burden of these piss-poor shenanigans has to fall somewhere, and for the most part it's on the heads of our publicists and agents; again, another reason I chose the hard-bitten, two-fisted, take-no-prisoners Hughesy as my personal consigliore.

Less forceful agents and publicists, however, still have long memories and lots of scar tissue. There is always one monster among the visiting literati, one writer so irredeemably vile that nobody wants to wrangle them. And for some reason they often seem to be crazy American crime-writing ladies. One such bestselling creature, put out that nobody would carry her bags for her, spent her entire visit complaining about the wretched food, and pissy coffee and the horror of being dragged to this shit hole at the end of the world. She even alienated her fellow bestselling Americans, with whom she had to share a platform, asking, in front of them, 'What I am doing on stage with these fucking nobodies?'

Another author of massively popular pot boilers used to insist that a peeled Mars Bar be readied for him in the Green Room, before he went on stage, while a female novelist, now dead, simply couldn't leave her room until some long-suffering publicist had given her swollen, blue-veined feet a good rub down.

None of this should put you off attending, of course, unless you fancy a career at the bottom of the food chain in the publishing industry. For you, as for us, the drunken, drug-addled dilettantes, the festival is all about the good times. And the foot rubs.

CONCLUSION

Still, should you even be doing this? Thinking about being a writer? In one sense – hell, in all sorts of ways – it's madness. The old world and its certainties are in violent derangement and collapse. Newspapers and magazines close every day. The venerable and ancient trade of book publishing is beset on all sides by the tyranny of the new. Ever more resources go to fewer and fewer commercial writers, while thousands of would-be scribblers emerge from university with a Master of Fine Arts degrees every semester. Why the hell would you give up a regular job for this Greek fucking tragedy?

Because it's great. Even when it doesn't work, it's great. Human beings seek meaning in the world. It is our glory and our curse. We can do no other. And we find that meaning most often in the stories we tell about the world. Storytellers, the curators of meaning, have held a special place in all cultures through all time. Not always to their own advantage. There is a reason the dictator, his arse freshly planted upon the presidential throne, sends his secret policeman after the writers and artists and journalists first. If he's a smart dictator he knows that in the long run they are likely to give him a hell of a lot more trouble than any disaffected colonels or generals. The latter can be bought off, co-opted into the regime. The writer and the artist ... not as easily. This doesn't mean that the ranks of the collaborators have never held an artist who traded integrity for security. Integrity, you might remember, tastes like sawdust. Security can be a big bowl of chocolate ice-cream. But artists as a class are mad. They cannot help themselves. They see the world differently to the way the world sees itself, or would like to be seen. If you've made it this far, you probably share this madness.

It is a particular type of insanity that will see you turn your back on a regular paycheck and the security of an ordered life. If you have this madness you will see your friends and contemporaries surpass you in all the banal but essential measures of everyday life. To them go the rewards of collaboration, appeasement and accommodation with the way things are. To you, the thin consolations of the road less travelled, the path cut by your own hand. It's not exactly blood, sweat, toil and tears, but it can sure as hell feel like that some days.

I can't guarantee you success. I cannot even guarantee my own success. I can only promise you that if you do this, you put yourself at the very centre of the human story because it is there and only there that the storyteller can live.

Good luck.

... AND GET BACK TO YOUR FUCKING DEADLINE.

SOURCES

Rachel Aaron, personal website: rachelaaron.net.

E. Jean Carroll, *Hunter: The Strange and Savage Life of Hunter S. Thompson*, Plume, 1993.

Dave Eggers, *Zeitoun*, Penguin Books, 2011.

Don DeLillo, 'The Art of Fiction no. 135', *The Paris Review*, Fall 1993.

Neil Gaiman, personal blog: journal.neilgaiman.com.

Stephen King, *On Writing*, Hodder & Stoughton, 2012.

Hilary Mantel, as quoted in 'Ten Rules for Writing Fiction (Part Two)', *The Guardian*, 20 Feb., 2010.

Richard Morgan, *The Steel Remains*, Orion Publishing, 2009.

Marcel Proust, *Remembrance of Things Past*, Wordsworth Editions, 2006.

Leigh Sales, *Detainee 002: The case of David Hicks*, Melbourne University Press, 2007.

Karen Thompson Walker, *The Age of Miracles*, Simon & Shuster, 2013.

David Weber, *Off Armageddon Reef*, Pan Macmillan, 2011.

Tom Wolfe, *The New Journalism*, Pan Macmillan, 1975.

Charlotte Wood (ed.) 'The Writer's Room Interviews' 2013–2015. charlottewood.com.au/writers-room-interviews.htm.

William Zinsser, *On Writing Well: The classic guide to writing nonfiction,* 30th anniversary edition. HarperCollins, 2006.